Hatteras Island

KEEPER
of the
OUTER
BANKS

Also by Ray McAllister

Wrightsville Beach: The Luminous Island

Topsail Island: Mayberry by the Sea

*Reflections: Objects in Mirror Appear
Backwards, But Maybe It's Me*

JOHN F. BLAIR, PUBLISHER
WINSTON-SALEM, NORTH CAROLINA

Hatteras Island

KEEPER

of the

OUTER

BANKS

by RAY McALLISTER

JOHN F. BLAIR
PUBLISHER
1406 Plaza Drive
Winston-Salem, North Carolina 27103
www.blairpub.com

Manufactured in the United States of America

Cover image by Vicki McAllister
Map by Roy Wilhelm
Book design by Debra Long Hampton

Background photo on pages ii - iii, Carolina Power and
Light Photograph Collection, North Carolina State Archives

Background photo on page v by Vicki McAllister

Background photo on pages vi - vii, U. S. Air Force

Background photo on pages viii - ix by Vicki McAllister

Library of Congress Cataloging-in-Publication Data

McAllister, Ray, 1952–
Hatteras Island : keeper of the Outer Banks / by Ray McAllister.
p.   cm.
Includes bibliographical references and index.
ISBN 978-0-89587-364-4 (hardcover : alk. paper)—ISBN 978-0-89587-363-7
(pbk. : alk. paper) 1. Hatteras Island (N.C.)—History. I. Title.

F262.096M34 2009
975.6'1—dc22   2009004629

www.blairpub.com

For Ryan

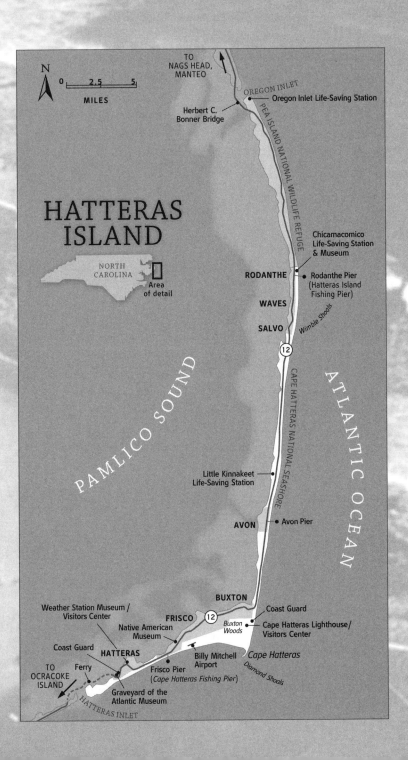

N

0   2.5   5
MILES

TO
NAGS HEAD,
MANTEO

OREGON INLET

Oregon Inlet Life-Saving Station

Herbert C.
Bonner Bridge

HATTERAS
ISLAND

NORTH
CAROLINA

Area
of detail

PEA ISLAND NATIONAL WILDLIFE REFUGE

Chicamacomico
Life-Saving Station
& Museum

RODANTHE ● Rodanthe Pier
(Hatteras Island
Fishing Pier)

WAVES

SALVO

12

Wimble Shoals

PAMLICO SOUND

CAPE HATTERAS NATIONAL SEASHORE

ATLANTIC OCEAN

Little Kinnakeet
Life-Saving Station

AVON ● Avon Pier

BUXTON

Weather Station Museum /
Visitors Center

FRISCO

12

Coast Guard

Native American
Museum

Buxton
Woods

Cape Hatteras Lighthouse/
Visitors Center

Coast Guard   HATTERAS

TO
OCRACOKE
ISLAND

Ferry

Billy Mitchell
Airport

Cape Hatteras

Frisco Pier
(Cape Hatteras Fishing Pier)

Diamond Shoals

Graveyard of the
Atlantic Museum

HATTERAS INLET

Contents

Preface

Our first year, we went to the wrong place.

It was so good that we kept going back.

This was September 1982, after Labor Day, when we labored our way down North Carolina Highway 12 past the crowded islandopolis of Kitty Hawk, Kill Devil Hills, and Nags Head, which was where most sensible people from Richmond stopped on North Carolina's Outer Banks. Back then, going even that far was a four-hour drive. But I had seen Nags Head a decade earlier and liked it better the way it had been, so we kept going onto Hatteras Island. Vicki and I and our infant daughter, Lindsay, accompanied by a collapsible playpen, were headed to an Outer Banks unencumbered by fast-food restaurants, shopping centers, and motel chains.

What lay ahead, we weren't quite sure. We drove down the narrow highway in the dark for another hour and a half, usually between lines of sand dunes that made it seem a slalom course, looking for an inexpensive motel near the Cape Hatteras Lighthouse. The lighthouse was the only spot we knew of. We drove almost to the end of the island, finally reaching little Hatteras Village. We stopped at the Sea Gull Motel and checked in for the night.

In the morning, we discovered the lighthouse was in the village of Buxton, 15 miles behind us. Three towns, in fact, were closer to it than was Hatteras Village.

We stayed nonetheless, willing to forgive the island that small deceit. The island reciprocated generously. September on Hatteras Island is a glorious time. The weather and the water retain summer's warmth. Prices have dropped from the peak season, and crowds have dwindled now that school has started—not that the island is ever really crowded.

We went back the next year and the next and the next. September on Hatteras is absolutely glorious—unless a hurricane or a nor'easter is coming, of course, in which case it is absolute hell.

One year, we did get caught at the Sea Gull in a tropical storm. The electricity went out. The world crashed down around us. A Hatteras storm in the middle of the night is sheer terror. The next morning, the little-used island road was filled with people leaving.

But that was the exception. Cares wash away on Hatteras. Wristwatches lose their function. Each September morning for four years, we would walk across the main road—scarcely having to look, so infrequently were cars coming—to a breakfast spot called The Lightship Restaurant. We might find two other couples there. We might find no one. Likewise, we had the beach and the few shops almost to ourselves. Hatteras visitors were more apt to be fishermen than tourists that time of year.

We always stayed at the Sea Gull. By then, our son, Ryan, had been born. If we were going to arrive late, the motel people would tape the room key to the office door. The allure of Hatteras was always the same. The allure was . . . nothing. Adventures on the island were few—a trip to the lighthouse, buying T-shirts, a cookout on the beach, afternoon storms. Oh, and I once had to yank Lindsay from the surf so forcefully her arm was in a sling for several days. The Hatteras undertow is not to be trifled with.

We left the island before our younger daughter, Jamie, was born. Lindsay had started school, and Septembers on Hatteras were no longer an option. The realization brought sadness.

But the island remained on our minds. In 1990, I wrote a column about Hatteras for the *Richmond Times-Dispatch*. A dredge, buffeted during a heavy storm, had knocked out the bridge to the island. I called down to the Sea Gull to talk to one of the owners, Katie Oden, who said Outer Banks people were used to that sort of thing. "The people down here, I don't want to say it's not an inconvenience, because it is, but it's not something you're not at all ready for," Katie said, using up her share of negatives.

Thirteen years later, I called the Sea Gull for another column and reached Katie again. This time, Hurricane Isabel had devastated Hatteras. The Sea Gull itself was national news. Part of the motel had been deposited across the street, part was sitting in the middle of the main highway, and Rooms 5 through 10 had simply been demolished.

But Marci, the daughter of Katie and Jeff Oden, was the main concern. She had been trapped inside the motel as chest-high water blocked the doors. Finally, the ocean smashed through a window and carried her into a motel garage. She got into the attic. Her parents prayed. "We were absolutely positive that she didn't make it. She was trapped," Katie said over the phone. "Our prayers were answered." Jeff and a neighbor waded to the motel with a surfboard to steady themselves. Jeff carried his exhausted daughter to safety.

Katie Oden said the damage was estimated at $3 million

and the motel would not reopen. That was no easy decision for the two. Katie had been on the island for 30 years at that point, and Jeff was a seventh-generation Hatterasman.

But there is something in the Hatteras spirit. More than two decades after we had last seen the island, Vicki and I returned. We were looking to do a follow-up book to earlier ones on Topsail Island and Wrightsville Beach, and we had no doubt where we would go. We took that long drive down Hatteras—and came upon the Sea Gull again. Some of the destroyed portion had been rebuilt. The motel was open. On the wall was a framed front page of the Norfolk *Virginian-Pilot* featuring Isabel's wrath upon the Sea Gull.

To say Hatteras is unchanged would be lying. It has changed. But it has changed little—far less than most other resorts—and it has kept its soul. That may be more nature's doing than man's. Man wins many contests elsewhere, but here, on Hatteras Island, put your money on nature.

The book that has emerged here is neither a travel guide nor a history nor a paean to a disappearing lifestyle, though it contains elements of each. It is certainly not the definitive book on Hatteras Island. That book has never been written and never will be. Indeed, anyone who trifles with the history of Hatteras runs the risk of getting it so intertwined with legend, hearsay, and errors of fact as to be unrecognizable. One islander, referring to non-locals who would write Hatteras history, says bluntly, "They hear these stories and they think they know who the people are and they put it together, and it's the greatest mess you ever heard when it comes out."

This book is, instead, a conversation with an island.

It is shared memories with a warm beach, recollections of a storm, tales from a violent ocean. It is hot July days and dreary February days and the promising days of early May. It is wind and rain and sunrises and sunsets and blowing sand and churning surf and you'd-better-be-ready-when-the-storm-hits-because-it-ain't-waitin'-for-you. Count on that, my friend. It is long-dead fishermen and lifesavers peering out from old photographs, and tourists and kite boarders smiling from new ones, and natives and transplants brought together every summer, the latter sometimes charmed by the former and the former simply putting up with the latter until finally, by God, they leave. All share and celebrate this ever-changing—ever-*challenging*—spit of land that nobody should be able to live on. But don't you dare try to tell them they shouldn't be here. They would be no place else.

Pull up a chair. Have a listen.

Hatteras Island

KEEPER
of the
OUTER
BANKS

Chapter One
KEEPER OF THE OUTER BANKS

The Outer Banks of North Carolina are not of North Carolina at all. Any minimally detailed map, let alone a satellite view from space, shows they belong to the Atlantic Ocean, as much a part of the sea as fish and waves, and as much at the sea's mercy as sandcastles on the beach. This is particularly true of Hatteras Island, a 50-mile-long piece of dental floss constantly being redefined by wind and wave.

Tourists and developers long ago discovered the island, a spit of land that looks like an eastward-billowing sail. Much has changed on Hatteras as a result. Even more, however, has not. Elsewhere, fast-food restaurants, strip malls, and beach-dominating duplexes have overcome resort islands, including the more northern reaches of the Outer Banks. But the storm-buffeted Hatteras—with an average width of just two-thirds of a mile, often just five feet above sea level, as much as 30 miles from the mainland, and largely

protected against intruders by national seashore status—
has kept its soul.

The Outer Banks soul is a complicated matter. Many
acknowledge there is such a thing. Few, however, agree on
what it is.

It is obvious that geography and the elements have
pounded their imprint on it. Tom Carlson, in his book *Hatteras Blues*, puts it this way: "Early on, especially, it seems,
the inhabitants of the Outer Banks didn't merely adapt to
their environment; they became indistinguishable from it—
its moody, impetuous weather, its restless land, its willful-
ness, its stubborn insistence on beating the odds."

The Outer Banks soul may well go back to the earliest settlers, Native Americans and Englishmen both, hardy
souls who persevered even when God surely must have been
having a laugh at their expense. It may go back to the Civil
War, when, turning their backs on the rest of North
Carolina, islanders were more supportive of the Union
army than the Confederate because the federal government
had always supported them. Or it may go back to the earliest
keepers. Keepers of the lighthouse. Keepers of the lightship.
Keepers of the lifesaving stations. They had tasks. They had
responsibilities. They had duties.

The Hatteras soul has something to do with the icono-
clastic nature of families who have lived on the island for
generations, if not centuries. It has to do with the spirit of
vacationers who would rather come to a run-down cottage
or a two-star motel than to a luxury resort elsewhere. It has
to do with the virtual inaccessibility of the island for much
of its history and, even now, with the difficulty of traveling
its length. It has to do with tolerating, even embracing, isolation and loneliness. It has to do with surf and wind and
sun and living an outdoor life, whether it be that of wizened
commercial fishermen who have worked the waters for a

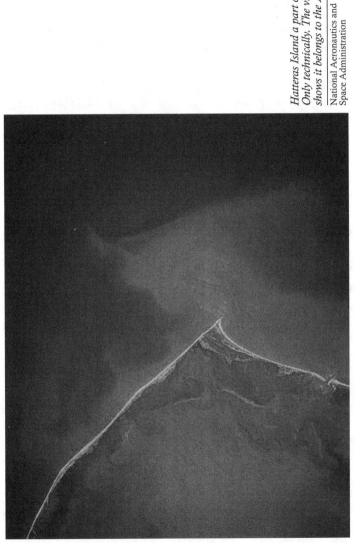

Hatteras Island a part of North Carolina? Only technically. The view from space shows it belongs to the Atlantic Ocean.

National Aeronautics and Space Administration

half-century, forty-something off-roaders, or teenage kite boarders. It has to do with finding value in everyday activities that might bemuse others. It has to do with not caring if others are bemused.

A local preacher, speaking of religion, though it could have been almost anything, not long ago gave an assessment of islanders that cut across denominational boundaries. "They're fatalists," he said. "They believe that their life here is a gift from God. If you were to say to them, 'There's a 90 percent chance that a tidal wave is coming in the next 10 years, and it's going to demolish this island,' they'd go, 'I don't want to live anywhere else.' If they were Pentecostals, they'd say, 'I'll just stay prayed up, honey!' Methodists will say, 'I hope everything will be all right!' They're going to live here until the end."

One might credit, too, Cape Hatteras National Seashore, which takes up two-thirds of the island, blocking construction within its boundaries and effectively limiting it elsewhere. The type of ever-expanding sprawl seen elsewhere cannot get a strong foothold on Hatteras. The long drives required to get from one town to another discourage a crushing influx of tourists and builders. Without the seashore, it is a virtual certainty that much of the island would have been developed. Many credit the seashore, though many also blame it for trying to take over. Those on Hatteras want few restraints.

Hatteras has remained Hatteras, even if here and there a Wings T-shirt emporium has popped up. Gee Gee Rosell, a local shop owner, credits the weather, in part. "It changes every day," she says. "The Weather Channel is my favorite television station. I probably wouldn't have a television if I didn't watch the Weather Channel."

Oh, yes. The weather. Weather changes are everyone's number-one topic on Hatteras, television set or not, and with good reason. Malevolent storms whip themselves up quickly and strike with frightening dispatch. Have you never been caught in one?

A July visitor to the island goes for a morning beach walk, heading northward along the water line. Nothing suggests anything but a glorious start to the day. The newly arrived sun glistens on the water to the visitor's right, and those waves roll in and over his bare feet. The breeze is welcoming. Sea gulls laugh overhead. Fellow beach walkers smile, some stopping to say hello, most just nodding before quickly returning to their relentless scan of the sand for the perfect shell or piece of sea glass brought in by the overnight surf. There is no better place to be than here on Hatteras Island this morning. Three miles of walking go quickly.

Nearly reaching the fishing pier at Rodanthe, the visitor chances to take a look backward. A storm has been charging up behind him, from the south. Already, it blackens the sky. The wind has kicked up. He should have noticed. A few beach walkers seem momentarily unconcerned or, more likely, unaware. Most, however, are picking up their pace. The man turns back into the approaching storm, increasing his own pace. Raindrops begin to fall. Off in the distance, lightning appears over the ocean, flashing downward from cloud to wave.

Five minutes later, the pelting raindrops are strong enough to sting. The air is cooler. The wind is rougher. The sand, so inviting to walk upon minutes earlier, now slows every effort to make good time. The man's T-shirt is soaked. His leg muscles begin to tire. Other beach walkers, facing shorter distances, have become runners, or at least leaners into the wind. Urgency defines their movements. Many cut across the upper beach diagonally, seeking the wooden steps that will take them up and over the dunes to their cottages.

Lightning moves closer. It dives into the ocean on the

left again and reaches down to the land on the right as well. The beach, for the moment, seems almost a safety zone between the two expanses of electricity.

The beach, however, is no place to be. The evacuation of early-morning walkers and fishermen has quickened. Even the gulls have gone. The sands have become virtually empty as far as the visitor can see in the driving rain. If something were to happen to him, he muses, no one would find his body in time to help. He moves up to the next crossover, smiling at his motivation, falling in behind the last four people to leave this stretch of beach. Lightning flashes nearby, the thunder exploding immediately on top of the flash. The group chatters excitedly, nervously, walks faster, then breaks into a trot. Soon, the four peel off at a cottage, safe.

The visitor continues as the rain drives harder, catching up to a group of three college students, who in turn drop off a block later. The streets, lined with cottages, are now empty. It is the height of the summer season. It may as well be the dead of winter. No one is about. The rain beats harder. The lightning continues.

It will be nearly half an hour before the visitor, half-walking, half-jogging, reaches his room safely—and thankfully. He makes a mental note never again to take the Hatteras weather for granted.

The point is, this was not an extraordinary Hatteras storm in any sense. Dozens, scores, perhaps even a hundred storms are as bad each year. Many are extraordinary. Drownings are not uncommon. Nor are summer lightning strikes. Lightning took the life of an 18-year-old sitting on the beach near the Cape Hatteras Lighthouse in 1997. It killed a 26-year-old woman in a Hatteras parking lot in 2002.

Such weather is all too familiar to those of the island, going back to the Native Americans who preceded recorded history. Pirates were caught unaware, and fishermen, too, just as beachgoers and surfers and kite boarders are today. Any storm on the island is a sea storm, whether a rainstorm or an electrical storm, a windstorm or an ice storm, a nor'easter or a hurricane. They are all storms of the Atlantic Ocean. You may not have a boat. But on Hatteras, you are always at sea.

A Union soldier stationed on Hatteras during the Civil War described the difficulty of merely pitching a tent: "To have a tent prove false [on] a lone, barren isle, and in the midst of a terrific rain storm, be obliged to face a Hatteras wind, with scant protection against the fury, frantically holding fast to the frail canvas house, waiting for a lull in the blast (vain hope) to afford an opportunity to repeg, is so overpoweringly harrowing to the feelings, and so indescribably uncomfortable, that it is only those who actually experienced it who understand its supreme misery."

The keepers of the Cape Hatteras Lighthouse and the lifesaving stations up and down the island knew as well as anyone of these nasty turns of weather, of the dangers that sprang up instantly. Theirs was a job of warning and protection.

It was no easy job to be a lighthouse keeper. From the earliest days, the task was carried out in loneliness, isolation, and brutal weather. Merely keeping the light on for passing ships was difficult. The light consisted of a lamp with a lighted wick, amplified by a lens. The keeper had to keep the wick constantly trimmed and supplied with whale oil, lard, rapeseed, and, later, petroleum products. The lens had to be kept soot-free. Many keepers were former sailors themselves. Others were women. All shared a difficult duty. There was no taking the day off for bad weather.

Above all, then, is the indomitable spirit of the people of the island themselves. Hatterasmen and Hatteraswomen have proven more hardy than most people through the years. They have had to. Theirs has been a life of the sea and the wind, cut off from the lifelines available to everyone else. Anything they wanted, they had to fight for.

Then they had to keep it.

Chapter Two
BEGINNINGS

Most of Hatteras Island's inhabitation by humans, of course, has been by Native Americans. The Croatan tribe of the Algonquin Indians is believed to have been on the island since about 500 A.D. Indeed, the word *Hatteras* is an English rendition of an Algonkian word meaning "there is less vegetation." The name, originally spelled *Hatorask*, was applied by Sir Walter Raleigh's colonists to what became the Chicamacomico area, near where the island's three northernmost villages now lie.

Fishing and hunting abounded on Hatteras Island. Archaeologists believe the natives occupied a large area at what are now Frisco and Buxton, including Buxton Woods. A large shell repository and trash heap was found in Frisco, suggesting they ate oysters and clams.

Not far from the spot now, in a low-slung building that suddenly appears around a bend on Highway 12, is the Frisco Native American Museum and Natural History Center. Much of the building is more than a century old itself, having been a general store, gathering place, post office, and shell shop.

Much of what it displays, of course, is older yet. Carl

Different inlets define it today, but Hatteras Island still is instantly recognizable in this portion of a 1590 map. What is now the island was divided roughly into thirds on the White-De Bry map. From north to south are Hattorask, Paquiwoc, and Croatoan. To the south is Wokokon, an island thought to consist of the lower half of what is now Ocracoke Island. This Theodor De Bry map engraving was based on drawings by John White.

National Park Service

and Joyce Bornfriend, both educators, keep alive the voice of the Native Americans in a unique setting. Artifacts come from the first inhabitants of the island, as well as from tribes across the United States. The couple's museum opened in 1986. Its exhibits have expanded a bit at a time through the small, low-ceilinged rooms and into new space. A nature trail and a pavilion have been added, along with a research facility and a gift shop.

"The museum was started by my concern to preserve the Native American experience," says Carl Bornfriend, the director and curator. Bornfriend is from Philadelphia, where his father was a furrier, making coats for the likes of Princess Grace, Bette Davis, and Eleanor Roosevelt—and instructing his son to respect all peoples. At an early age, Bornfriend became concerned with portrayals of Native Americans and the casual indifference shown to their artifacts. He soon became a collector. "My family is military," he says matter-of-factly. "I would trade military stuff for Native American stuff."

The collection has grown beyond Bornfriend's own artifacts. But one of the museum's most noteworthy pieces was found on its own property—a dugout canoe buried out back. The canoe is displayed with tools, instruments, and other items found in archaeological digs on the island.

Too little still is known about Native American life on the island. Glimpses, however, have appeared over the centuries.

In 1524, Italian navigator Giovanni da Verrazano, sailing for France, anchored off the North Carolina coast on the Feast of the Annunciation. "We called it Annunciata from the day of arrival, and found there an isthmus one mile wide and about two hundred miles long, in which we could see the eastern sea from the ship," Verrazano reported back to King Francis I.

The isthmus was part of the Outer Banks, apparently between Cape Hatteras and Cape Lookout. The so-called eastern sea, which he said "doubtless" led around the tip of India and China—a faulty supposition that led to a century-and-a-half perception that only the Outer Banks stood between the Atlantic and Pacific oceans—became known as "Verrazano's Sea." That sea was what we now know as Pamlico Sound, lying between the Outer Banks and the North Carolina mainland.

Despite Verrazano's error, his report to the king is an important document. It includes his description of this remarkable meeting likely near what is now Hatteras Village:

> All along [the coast] we saw great fires because of the numerous inhabitants; we anchored off the shore, since there was no harbor, and because we needed water we sent the small boat ashore with XXV men. The sea along the coast was churned up by enormous waves because of the open beach, and so it was impossible to put anyone ashore without endangering the boat. We saw many people on the beach making various friendly signs, and beckoning us ashore; and there I saw a magnificent deed, as Your Majesty will hear.
>
> We sent one of our young sailors swimming ashore to take the people some trinkets, such as little bells, mirrors, and other trifles, and when he came within four fathoms of them, he threw them the goods and tried to turn back, but he was so tossed about by the waves that he was carried up onto the beach half dead. Seeing this, the native people immediately ran up; they took him by the head, the legs, and arms and carried him some distance away. Whereupon the youth, realizing he was being carried away like this, was seized with terror, and began to utter loud cries. They answered him in their language to show him he should not be afraid. Then they placed him on the ground in the sun, at the foot of a small hill, and made gestures of great admiration, looking at the

whiteness of his flesh and examining him from head to foot. They took off his shirt and shoes and hose, leaving him naked, then made a huge fire next to him, placing him near the heat. When the sailors in the boat saw this, they were filled with terror, as always when something new occurs, and thought the people wanted to roast him for food.

After remaining with them for a while, he regained his strength, and showed them by signs that he wanted to return to the ship. With the greatest kindness, they accompanied him to the sea, holding him close and embracing him; and then to reassure him, they withdrew to a high hill and stood watching him until he was in the boat.

Spanish and then English explorers next visited the North Carolina coast. The English, under the direction of Sir Walter Raleigh, made a strong attempt to colonize the area in the 1580s, setting up a fort on Roanoke Island and mapping Cape Hatteras as "Hattorask."

The famed Lost Colony, whose inhabitants disappeared and were rumored killed, may well have fled to Hatteras Island and the friendly Croatan Indians instead. The letters *CRO* and the name *CROATOAN* were found carved in trees nearby. Some later proof came in what appears to have been the mixing of European and Native American genes. (Indeed, Kinnakeet, the early name for Avon, means "land of the mixed.") Englishman John Lawson, writing in 1709, relied in part on the Croatans—by that time called the Hatteras Indians—for the following assessment nearly a century and a half after the fact: "These tell us that several of their ancestors were white people, and could talk in a book [read], as we do; the truth of which is confirmed by gray eyes being found frequently amongst these Indians, and no others."

A Native American midden, or refuse heap, was unearthed

The Frisco Native American Museum holds some of the answers to the island's earliest and least-known peoples.

Photograph by Vicki McAllister

near Buxton by Hurricane Emily in 1993. It contained mollusk shells, animal bone fragments, and pottery pieces, suggesting it was a central location of the Croatans, a Carolina Algonkian society believed to have lived on Hatteras from about 800 to 1700. Archaeologists made headlines when they reported finding gun flints, copper farthings, brass pins, and a 16th-century English gold signet ring.

As had Native Americans, early European settlers on the island mostly fished, both for subsistence and to trade with mainland plantations for corn. They also butchered whales and dolphins that came ashore and took the cargoes and timbers of wrecked ships. Some thought they were land pirates who lured ships to ruin by setting up false lights and markers. The historical evidence suggests they were merely opportunists. Claiborne Snead, a Confederate colonel during the Civil War, wrote that Hatteras was

> inhabited by a class of people who subsist by fishing and hunting as well as from cargoes of vessels stranded upon the stormy coast. They are commonly called "wreckers" and seem to do a lucrative business, from the numberless wrecks scattered along the beach. . . .
>
> The islanders mingle little with the outside world; apparently indifferent to the outside sphere, they constitute a world within themselves.

Indeed, families tended to stay put generation after generation. Most local names from the late 1700s still appeared in the 1860 census, and many remain on the island. The harsh environment also was a defining feature. A Union soldier from Pennsylvania wrote, "Hatteras Island was, and possibly still is, inhabited by a hardy, raw-boned, tough looking people, with rough, weather beaten countenances, and possessed of a good stock of native shrewdness. There are few deaths among them, the chief disease is consumption. . . . The women are pale, frail, attenuated creatures who apparently never grow old. Tradition has it that they gradually shrink up, and at some remote period are blown away."

Union soldiers stationed on the island during the Civil War intermingled with the population, buying fish and sometimes dating local women—and then writing home about their "dreadful habit of snuff-dipping." One Northern soldier gave a thorough description of typical mid-19th-century life on the island:

> Quite a number of houses have a "grandfather's clock" ticking in the corner, or back of the door. The display of furniture is not extensive—indeed, it is generally scarce; pieces of wrecks and ship stock have to answer the purpose. The staple articles of food are fish and sweet potatoes. Corn, pigs and poultry are raised by some. Garden cultivation is very primitive and exceedingly careless. Some miserable oysters can be obtained and an occasional opossum. All of the sugar, coffee, tea, and molasses used by the natives come from wrecks. They are a religious people, in their peculiar way, vigorous in attendance at divine service and any infringement of the laws is tried in the church.

Outsiders today usually perceive Hatteras Island as one entity, bound by geography and defined by a way of life. But older islanders remember when little communities—it would be a stretch to call them villages—were decidedly separate. The old communities' names were maintained, at least informally, deep into the 20th century. Those living in what are now Rodanthe, Waves, and Salvo—sometimes called the Tri-Village—were Chicamacomicoers. Avon people were Kinnakeeters. Those in Frisco were called Trenters. Those in Hatteras Village were Hatterassers.

And residents of Buxton? Oddly enough, they were mostly called Billygoaters, an old-timer remembers. Or sometimes Goaters. Or even Capers or Sea Tickers. "I really don't know why that is," he says. "Evidently, there must have been goats down there."

Historically, the residents of Rodanthe and Waves were close, but the difficulty of getting from one village to another negated much contact among the others. The island was covered with sand, marshes, and thick woods, none of which was helpful to vehicular travel. Most commerce and even mail delivery was by boat. Here again, the Hatteras environment presented problems. Rough seas and quick-rising storms made water travel an uncertain proposition. Not until 1952 would the island have a highway that made travel more practical.

Because of flooding, homes were built on pilings. They had no basements, of course. "Not one house on the island enjoys this luxury, they cannot dig them," a Union soldier wrote. "The floors of many houses were sprinkled with fine white sand, which, with constant wear and friction, produces white smooth floors."

One surprising feature of the island was the ubiquitous windmills, usually used for grinding corn. Another Union soldier, Charles F. Johnson, wrote, "Everything on the Island seems devoid of paint—dwellings, barns, and windmills, of which latter there are a greater number than I supposed were in existence in the whole country."

Much of the history of Hatteras has been tied to fishing, whether by islanders feeding their families, commercial fishermen, or tourists and sportfishermen. The 1870 census showed that 60 percent of residents were fishermen.

Recent generations of commercial fishermen have gone after crabs in spring and summer and then dropped their nets for fish in the fall and early winter. Increasingly, however, they have been pushed from their occupation, whether by increased regulation or by fewer fishing opportunities

Corn-grinding windmills like this one at Buxton around 1900 once dotted Hatteras. "There are a greater number than I supposed were in existence in the whole country," wrote a Union soldier stationed on the island.

Photograph by H. H. Brimley, North Carolina State Archives

as development and tourism have expanded. Hunting, too, was once a part of nearly every islander's life but has now been restricted.

Until the 20th century, one leftover from the earliest days lingered: cows and horses ran free on the island, some belonging to Hatteras families, some wild and unclaimed. Anyone wanting a ride simply caught a horse and rode it bareback. Children and adults often did that, though sometimes it wasn't an easy chore. One Buxton woman recalled the time she and her brother were sent after one of her father's mares with a bridle. The mare, Mary, was in heat. A stallion charged the two children. "We were both going to ride her bareback," she said. "But here comes this old stallion. He'd rare up on his hind legs and scream. Honey, that was two scared kids. You talking about somebody praying. We kept inching along until he ran back to his brood. We'd be a-crying, telling Dad about it. He said, 'Well, next time, I'll give you a gig and gig him like that.' And very calmly, Mother said, 'No, Jim. There won't be a next time.' "

Something else seems to have attached to the people of Hatteras through the generations: a deep appreciation for where they were. Nobody came to this place by accident. They made a choice.

This Hatteras native perhaps put it best: "Some of the old fishermen were very inarticulate. But they were experiencing the same things as a very articulate poet when they would see a sunset or a sunrise or a rainbow or storm. They were moved by that. And they didn't start gushing out with a bunch of words. But they'd say, 'Boy, that was some pretty.' "

One can say that often on Hatteras.

Boy, that was some pretty.

Chapter Three

PIRATES

I t is sometimes called "the Golden Age of Piracy" on the North Carolina coast—though the sentiment surely applied more to the pirates than to their victims—and for a noteworthy period, the Outer Banks were right in the middle of it.

The time was briefer than most people realize. While pirates were at sea between roughly 1630 and 1720, they operated off the Carolina coast mostly between 1713 and 1718 and seriously affected the Outer Banks for less than a year. That was more than enough, however.

Pirates had established operations throughout the Caribbean in the 17th century, but British naval forces eventually sent them scurrying. They moved to the coasts of North and South America. Several set up operations in North Carolina. "Carolina's isolated backwaters provided perfect haven for the vagabond pirates," writes Lindley S. Butler in *Pirates, Privateers, and Rebel Raiders of the Carolina Coast*. "Equally appealing was the weak authority of proprietary officials, the sparse settlement, and the relative poverty of the colony. A low volume of trade and a subsistence economy meant fewer customs collectors and a government willing to accommodate merchants or traders who could, by dealing with smugglers and pirates, offer an abundance of low-priced goods."

The Carolina pirates, writes David Stick in *Graveyard of the Atlantic*, "rendezvoused behind the isolated islands of the Outer Banks, sailed out from there to attack merchant vessels, then returned again to celebrate and fight over their loot and maybe even bury some of it behind the ever-shifting dunes. Between them, the pirates were as much a menace for a time as the winds and tides and shoals."

Those pirates included Thomas Paine, Christopher Moody, John Cole, Robert Deal, Charles Vane, Richard Worley, John "Calico Jack" Rackham, Anne Bonny, Stede Bonnet, Francis Farrington Spriggs—and, of course, Blackbeard.

Blackbeard was possibly born Edward Drummond, more possibly Edward Teach or Ned Teach, and perhaps most likely Edward Thatch . . . or Thach . . . or Thache . . . or Tash. His early life is equally unclear. He is most often said to have been born in Bristol, England—though sometimes in London or Jamaica or even Philadelphia. North Carolina author, historian, and filmmaker Kevin P. Duffus introduced yet another possibility in his 2008 book, *The Last Days of Black Beard the Pirate*—namely, that he was actually Edward "Black" Beard, born near Charleston, South Carolina, and brought to North Carolina by his father.

Regardless, Blackbeard quickly earned a place among the most successful and most notorious of pirates. Most of what we know about him—at least the popular perception—comes from *A General History of the Pyrates* by Captain Charles Johnson (who some say was the novelist Daniel Defoe), published six years after Blackbeard's death.

Blackbeard, portrayed here in an engraving published shortly after his death, ter-rorized the North Carolina coast before meeting his end at Ocracoke Inlet, south of Hatteras. Did the pirate stride Hatteras Island itself? Quite possibly, but like Blackbeard's true name and even his birthplace, nothing is certain.

From *A General History of the Pyrates* by Captain Charles Johnson, 1724

"Captain Johnson may have done as much for Thatch's larger-than-life image as did the rogue himself," Butler writes.

Johnson's imagery was indeed colorful. He wrote that Blackbeard took the name, along with his appearance, to enhance his reputation for evil:

> Our Heroe, Captain *Teach*, assumed the Cognomen of *Black-beard*, from that large Quantity of Hair, which, like a frightful Meteor, covered his whole Face, and frightened *America* more than any Comet that has appeared there a long Time.
>
> This Beard was black, which he suffered to grow of an extravagant Length; as to Breadth, it came up to his Eyes; he was accustomed to twist it with Ribbons, in small Tails . . . and turn them about his Ears: In Time of Action, he wore a Sling over his Shoulders, with three brace of Pistols, hanging in Holsters like Bandaliers; and stuck lighted Matches under his Hat, which appearing on each Side of his Face, his Eyes naturally looking fierce and wild, made him altogether such a Figure, that Imagination cannot form an Idea of a Fury, from Hell, to look more frightful.

Blackbeard earned his reputation by deed as well. He invited his crew members to play high-stakes games of what might today be called "brinksmanship" or just "chicken," as Johnson related:

> In the Common wealth of Pyrates, he who goes the greatest Length of Wickedness, is looked upon with a kind of Envy amongst them, as a Person of a more extraordinary Gallantry, and is thereby entitled to be distinguished by some Post, and if such a one has but Courage, he must certainly be a great Man. The Hero of whom we are writing, was thoroughly accomplished this Way, and some of his Frolicks of Wickedness, were so extravagant, as if he aimed at making his Men believe he was a Devil

incarnate; for being one Day at Sea, and a little flushed with drink:—*Come*, says he, *let us make a Hell of our own, and try how long we can bear it*; accordingly he, with two or three others, went down into the Hold, and closing up all the Hatches, filled several Pots full of Brimstone, and other combustible Matter, and set it on Fire, and so continued till they were almost suffocated, when some of the Men cried out for Air; at length he opened the Hatches, not a little pleased that he held out the longest.

But it was on the high seas that Blackbeard's reputation was spread. He began pirating after 1713, perhaps as late as 1716, and terrorized the seas in 1717 and 1718. His men ruthlessly attacked merchant vessels, many off North Carolina, stealing goods and even the ships themselves. He killed some crew members in battle, taking others into his crew or setting them adrift. Though it is not known exactly how many vessels Blackbeard's men captured, a preliminary database compiled by researchers at the North Carolina Maritime Museum in Beaufort shows the number was more than 50.

Blackbeard apparently moved to the Carolina coast in the spring of 1718 with a fleet of four vessels and about 400 pirates, having captured a couple dozen ships and their valuable cargoes. He famously blockaded the harbor of Charleston, South Carolina, in May 1718, capturing eight or nine vessels over the course of a week, taking their goods, and ransoming the ships. Afterward, Blackbeard sank two of his own ships in Beaufort Inlet, marooning 17 of his most troublesome pirates on an uninhabited island. Then he sailed the coast to Ocracoke Inlet and later to Bath, where he apparently "retired," reputedly took a teenager as his 14th wife, and was granted amnesty by supportive North Carolina governor Charles Eden. In time, however, he went back to pirating from his Ocracoke base.

People underestimated the pirate at their peril, says Danny Couch, Hatteras Island historian and tour operator. "Blackbeard, he was a shrewd cat," Couch says, adding that "he [also] was a psychopath, an outlaw, a criminal."

Blackbeard had the advantage at sea. He would sail from Ocracoke toward Cape Hatteras, Couch says, and overtake ships that already had enough worries. "Riding the Gulf Stream north, you had to be careful on Diamond Shoals," steering far enough east to avoid running aground, Couch explains. "Now, here he comes. He kind of had you boxed in."

Blackbeard found himself in the right place at the right time. "Ocracoke Inlet was handling the entire economy of North Carolina," Couch says. While historical details are sketchy, "it's inevitable [traders] were dealing with Blackbeard. The guy had access to stuff that was much in demand—cocoa, chocolate, coffee, tea, foodstuffs, spices, luxury items, clothing, various shipping items. . . . He was money to the Hatteras islanders and the Ocracoke islanders—the 'Bankers,' they were called. They weren't the Outer Banks yet. They were called 'the Sand Banks.' "

Blackbeard was not alone at Ocracoke. Records show that a number of pirates gathered for a days-long party in the early fall of 1718. "Five of the most notorious pirates were gathered down there," Couch says. Those pirates were Blackbeard, the murderous Charles Vane, Calico Jack Rackham, Israel Hands (one of Blackbeard's navigators), and Robert Deal. Blackbeard's bodyguard, Caesar, was also present.

The party came to the attention of Virginia governor Alexander Spotswood, who at the behest of North Carolinians leery of their own governor's motives sent a Royal Navy contingent to take the pirate. Blackbeard was killed during a vicious battle—Butler calls it "the bloodiest six minutes ever fought on Carolina waters"—at Ocracoke Inlet on November 22, 1718. His throat was slashed, the fatal wound of the 25 on his body, five of which were delivered by pistol balls. Still, Blackbeard attempted to fight on. He had pulled a pistol from his belt and was beginning to cock it when he fell over dead on the deck. The victors affixed his severed head to the mast of their ship as proof of his death. Later, it was displayed on a stick in Virginia as a lesson to would-be pirates.

Blackbeard's legend grew larger still after his death. Within months, a teenaged Benjamin Franklin was hawking the ballad "A Sailor Song on the Taking of Teach or Blackbeard the Pirate" in the streets of Boston. The concluding stanza:

> And when we no longer can strike a blow,
> Then fire the magazine, boys, and up we go!
> It's better to swim in the sea below
> Than to swing in the air and feed the crow,
> Says jolly Ned Teach of Bristol.

The mythologizing had begun. It was furthered by the 1724 publication of Captain Charles Johnson's popular book. The story has continued through the ages. More than a century and a half after Blackbeard's demise, Robert Louis Stevenson adopted the name Israel Hands for a pirate in his 1883 adventure novel, *Treasure Island*. Filmmakers have featured Blackbeard repeatedly—in the 1952 movie *Blackbeard, the Pirate*, Disney's 1968 *Blackbeard's Ghost*, and a pair of 2006 made-for-TV movies, *Blackbeard* and *Blackbeard: Terror at Sea*, among many other productions.

On the Outer Banks, Blackbeard nearly rivals the Cape Hatteras Lighthouse when it comes to marketing. Look at a phone book and it may appear the pirate founded a hotel in Ocracoke (Blackbeard's Lodge) and a marina in Hatteras

Village (Teach's Lair). More surprising is Blackbeard's Miniature Golf in Nags Head. When did the man have time for miniature golf?

Pirates as a whole continue their influence up and down the Outer Banks, from the Pirate's Chest Gift Shop in Ocracoke to the Pirate's Cove Yacht Club & Marina in Manteo to Pirate's Moor Townhomes in Kill Devil Hills. The *Cap'n Clam* charter boat, based in Hatteras Village, promises a "pirate adventure" for all. And don't forget the Buccaneer Hotel in Kitty Hawk and the Jolly Roger Restaurant in Kill Devil Hills—or, if you prefer, the Jolly Roger Pub & Marina in Ocracoke.

Beyond his days at Ocracoke, however, it is unclear how much of a connection Blackbeard had to the rest of the Outer Banks. "Did Blackbeard ever set foot on [Hatteras] island? That remains to be seen," Couch says.

Hatteras and Ocracoke, as today, were separated by Hatteras Inlet, though the inlet was about five miles south of today's, he notes. (The inlet closed about a decade after Blackbeard's death, connecting the islands until a hurricane more than a century later split them for good.) The people of the two islands had considerable contact, however. "Hatteras at that time, there were some guys that were trading with Blackbeard," Couch says. Among them were William Rollinson, who lived near what is now Frisco, and Francis Farrow, an island boatbuilder. "Francis Farrow and William Rollinson, I'm confident, had contacts with him," he says. "John Jennette, probably."

Some islanders no doubt saw Blackbeard regularly. "Blackbeard was not a threat to local people," Couch says. "Everybody in the colony, if you were in a boat, you were running into Blackbeard." The pirate was after only big merchant ships, which often sailed under European flags.

Thus far, however, Couch admits, "we have no

documented evidence that Blackbeard was traipsing around Hatteras on foot."

Blackbeard has been the subject of uncommon research for a man dead for three centuries, however. More continues to be learned—including at the site of his sunken *Queen Anne's Revenge* in Beaufort Inlet—more books continue to be written, and more theories are advanced. It could well be that documented evidence of his Hatteras contacts will be discovered one day.

In the meantime, in the absence of fact, legend suffices just fine.

Chapter Four
THE GHOSTSHIP OF DIAMOND SHOALS

On Monday, January 31, 1921, by dawn's first light, surfman Clarence P. Brady of the Cape Hatteras Coast Guard Station looked into the ocean—and was shocked.

A five-masted schooner, all sails set for maximum speed, no name visible, was riding a sand bar on Diamond Shoals in front of him.

It would be days before rescuers could reach the vessel in the stormy seas. There, they would find an equally shocking sight: nothing. No crew. No belongings. Nothing was aboard save a six-toed cat.

Moreover, they found no explanation for any of it.

Ghost stories are a staple of the Outer Banks, as much a part of the landscape, nearly, as nor'easters, sand dunes, and a fish on the line. Perhaps the otherworldly tales are a function of the distant locale or the inhospitable environment, or of the realization that man on these islands is but a foil for events, or of the willingness and the need, both, to while away the time on a spit of land with little in the way of entertainment by figuring in some ghostly delights. Some of the stories seem highly unlikely. Others seem altogether fabricated.

But how to explain the *Carroll A. Deering*?

Locals call the *Deering* "the Ghostship of Diamond Shoals" now, usually running ghost ship into one word, as if an entirely new creation. It is a word to explain the inexplicable.

The setting was nearly a century ago, on the famed and infamous shoals just off Cape Hatteras, a location more inhospitable than any other on the North Carolina coast and more responsible than any other for the dire moniker "Graveyard of the Atlantic." The three-tiered diamond-shaped shoals—consisting of Hatteras Shoals, Inner Diamond, and Outer Diamond—extend at least 14 miles to sea. Here, too, the warm Gulf Stream meets the cold Labrador Current, helping form storms that move north and, of course, further contributing to the difficulties of navigation.

Many a ship has been wrecked here. Many a life has been lost.

The most mysterious of all Hatteras shipwrecks, however, remains the 1921 foundering of the *Carroll A. Deering*, at which surfman Brady was looking. None of the other wrecks had the series of oddly ominous signs beforehand, the traceless disappearance of its crew, the complete absence of provable explanations, the myriad theories afterward. Even today, answers are no more than guesses.

The story began with the launching of the glorious 255-foot schooner in April 1919 in Bath, Maine. The *Carroll A. Deering* was the pride of the G. C. Deering Company, named for the owner's son. Described as "a tremendous sailing ship," the *Deering* would prove all of that, sailing proudly

Hatteras Island

The majestic five-masted schooner Carroll A. Deering *was launched April 1919 in Bath, Maine. Less than two years later, it was found empty on the Hatteras coast. For nearly a century, myriad theories have attempted— without success—to explain what happened to the mysterious "Ghostship of Diamond Shoals."*

Photographer unknown, www.mainetoday.com

and often during the next 21 months.

During a 1920–21 coal-delivery trip to South America, however, events began to go awry. The captain fell ill, and he and his son, the first mate, left the ship early. The company substituted an experienced 66-year-old captain, Willis T. Wormell, and the trip to Rio de Janeiro was completed without event. But once there, Wormell met with an old friend and fellow captain. Wormell confided that he was concerned by his crew and especially his first mate, Charles McLellan, whom he considered a troublemaker. The two captains agreed that at least Wormell would be able to count on his engineer, Herbert Bates, a good man.

After unloading its cargo, the *Deering* left Rio for Maine in December 1920. In early January 1921, the ship stopped in Barbados for liberty and supplies. Drinking and fighting were apparently important parts of the recreation. True to form, first mate McLellan got drunk and was thrown in jail. The captain bailed him out, yet McLellan was overheard threatening Wormell's life. McLellan said he would get Wormell before the ship reached Norfolk, Virginia.

Under these uneasy circumstances, the *Deering* left Barbados on January 9.

Still more ominous signs lay ahead, though the captain could not have known. On January 25, just days before the *Deering* would reach the same area, the SS *Hewitt*, sailing a similar course, disappeared off the Carolina coast. Neither it nor its crew of 42 was ever heard from again.

The *Deering* headed into a particularly stormy few weeks in the Atlantic. On January 29, the schooner, sailing at a mere five knots, passed the Cape Lookout Lightship, 90 miles south of Hatteras. The lightship keeper, Thomas Jacobson, was disturbed by something else, however: "A man on board other than the captain hailed the lightship and reported that the vessel had lost both its anchors while riding out the gale south of Cape Fear and asked to be reported to its owners." Jacobson said the man, who called through a megaphone, was tall and thin and had reddish hair—and didn't speak, act, or look like an officer. He and the crew were standing on the quarterdeck, usually an area off-limits to the crew.

Jacobson couldn't relay the message immediately. The lightship's radio was out. But a short time later, a steamer passed and Jacobson hailed it with his ship's whistle, a whistle so piercing it could be heard for five miles. The steamer did not respond. Maritime law said it must stop for a lightship, but the steamer, whose name was not visible, simply kept going.

Late the next afternoon, the SS *Lake Elon* passed a five-masted schooner that its captain would later realize was the *Deering*. These two ships were about 25 miles from the lightship and a half-mile from each other. This time, it wasn't the men aboard but the ship's course that was disturbing. Captain Henry Johnson reported,

> There was nothing irregular to be seen on board this vessel but she was steering a peculiar course. She appeared to be steering for Cape Hatteras. . . . The lookout on the schooner should have sighted Cape Hatteras Light, also the Light Ship at Diamond Shoal a little later than we did but in plenty time to avoid going on shore as the weather was clear and cloudy with good visibility. There [were] a couple of more ships in the vicinity steering a course parallel with us which should have convinced the Captain of the schooner that he was steering a wrong course.

Nonetheless, the *Carroll A. Deering*, intentionally or not, with a captain or without, was headed straight for Diamond Shoals.

At 6:30 the next morning, Monday, January 31, 1921,

surfman Brady was startled to see the nameless ship, sails set, riding a sand bar. He put out a call for help.

Surfmen from the Cape Hatteras, Big Kinnakeet, Creeds Hill, and Hatteras Inlet stations quickly launched two surfboats. The tiny craft were overmatched, however. Again and again they tried, but the crashing seas kept them a quarter-mile or more from the ship. They could not even maneuver close enough to make out its name.

Keeper C. R. Hooper of the Big Kinnakeet station later reported that the schooner had been "driven up high on the shoal . . . in a boiling bed of breakers with all sails set as if abandon[ed] in a hurry." Keeper J. C. Gaskill of the Creeds Hill station reported, "She had been stripped of all life-boats and no sign of life [was] on board. . . . Crew has apparently left in own boats, as ladder was hanging over side."

Rescuers kept trying over the next few days, but the Hatteras seas kept them away. Keeper Baxter Miller and his Cape Hatteras crew got within 500 yards of the ship but saw no signs of a crew.

On Tuesday, the day after the schooner was spotted, the Coast Guard cutter *Seminole* arrived from Wilmington. Though it reached the stranded ship, its men were unable to board. The *Seminole* wired for information: "Request name stranded schooner and whereabouts of crew if known. *Seminole*."

Back came the answer: "Schooner name unknown whereabouts of crew unknown. Diamond Shoals Lightship."

The next morning, Wednesday, a Coast Guard cutter from Norfolk, the *Manning*, and a wrecking tug, the *Rescue*, joined in. The four Hatteras Coast Guard stations kept at their work. Again and again, rescuers attempted to get near, but the bad weather continued. Waves broke over the deck of the *Carroll A. Deering*. By Thursday, water breached its hull.

That afternoon, February 3, an article appeared in the newspaper of the boat's hometown. Sparing no words in its opening paragraph, the *Bath* (Maine) *Daily Times* reported,

NO NEWS RECEIVED OF MISSING CREW
Schooner *Carroll A. Deering* Remains on Sands Off
Cape Hatteras

No news had come today concerning the Bath built schooner *Carroll A. Deering* which was driven on Diamond Shoals off Hatteras Monday night except that the vessel is lying there with all sails set but a rough sea has prevented reaching the craft, although the revenue cutter *Seminole*, and a boat with a representative of an insurance company, are lying off hoping to get more information as to the craft's condition when the seas, which are very rough, abate sufficiently. . . .

The fate of Capt. W. B. Wormell of Portland who was in charge of the craft temporarily and the crew of 11 men who abandoned the schooner is unknown. . . .

One of the owners said . . . it was his opinion that the officers and crew were rescued by a passing vessel and that they will be heard from later. With heavy seas running on those dangerous shoals it was his belief that the schooner would prove a total loss.

By Thursday, February 4—the fourth day—the seas finally moderated enough for the 205-foot *Manning* to anchor nearby and lower a boat. At 10:30 A.M., Coast Guardsmen were able to board. They found that waves had ripped apart the seams of the *Deering*. Water was filling its hull. They had no hope of floating the vessel. The *Deering* would indeed be a total loss.

They had expected as much. But the surfmen were not prepared for the other mysterious sights.

None of the *Deering*'s crew or officers was aboard.

A hungry cat with six toes—some accounts say three

cats—was the only sign of life.

No personal belongings could be found.

The lifeboats were gone, and the ship's ladders were hanging over the side.

The anchors were missing. The steering gear was disabled. Red running lights, indicating a ship out of control, had been run up the mast.

The ship's chronometer, log, and navigational equipment were missing, along with some papers. Charts were scattered about the master's bathroom.

On January 23, notes on the ship's map had changed from Captain Wormell's distinctive handwriting to someone else's.

In the captain's cabin were three different pairs of boots, none of them Wormell's. The spare bed had been slept in.

In the galley, pea soup, spare ribs, and coffee had been laid out for a meal—and left.

Questions were many and answers few. The *Bath Daily Times* that afternoon, in a story headlined "Captain's Wife Doubts Schooner Is *Deering*," reported, "Mrs. Wormell at her home, 61 Lawn avenue, this city, said today that she was not inclined to accept the report that this derelict reported by the *Seminole* was the *Carroll A. Deering*. She believes that had the vessel been abandoned Capt. Wormell and the crew would have been heard from by this time as there are life saving coast guard crews all along the Diamond Shoal. She is anxiously awaiting some authentic word from Capt. Wormell."

The ship was indeed the *Deering*—that was quickly cleared up—but other aspects of the mystery deepened. The schooner's final days remained cloudy. The *Bath Daily Times* next reported,

MYSTERY SURROUNDS BATH BUILT VESSEL
CARROLL A. DEERING
Some Seafaring Men Are of Opinion Crew
May Have Mutinied

A cloud of mystery surrounds the Bath built schooner, *Carroll A. Deering*. . . .

What has become of her crew is the question of which seafaring men are pondering. Many think the crew was lost in the sea in an attempt to get ashore when the schooner went aground. She lies on the southwest corner of Diamond Shoals about a mile and a half from shore, and for three days after she was first sighted she was covered with a heavy veil of mist. . . .

One theory advanced is that the crew of the *Carroll A. Deering* mutinied while the vessel was at sea, and left her drifting with all her sails set, [although] the theory is a bare one.

Meanwhile, wreckers removed salvageable items and carried them to Hatteras for auction. The ship had been valued at $270,000.00 but brought just $866.75 at auction on February 2. That included $25.00 for the ship itself. Hatteras native Lee Robinson bought the *Deering*, apparently aware he would not be able to move it off the shoals but proud to claim ownership of the "ghostship." The remaining money came from the food and materials aboard. After 60 percent went to the salvagers and additional funds were paid for the wreck commissioner and advertising, just $333.36 was left for the Deering Company.

Carroll Deering, the son for whom the ship was named, came to own two pieces of the wreck: its fog bell and burgee. Friends bid on the 13-inch-wide, 50-pound metal bell. The burgee, or identification flag, was not part of the auction but was given as a gift. The flag, never unfurled after the original launch, remained in excellent condition.

Later in February, the wreck was further battered by a severe storm, declared a menace to navigation, and dynamited. Timbers floated ashore on Hatteras, and part of the bow reached Ocracoke Island.

Now, it was time to discover what had happened. An extensive federal investigation began, pushed by Wormell's family and friends and a United States senator. Secretary of Commerce Herbert Hoover assigned his assistant, Lawrence Richey, to lead the investigation. Over time, five departments—Commerce, Justice, Treasury, Navy, and State—became involved.

Meanwhile, ocean searches continued into March. No sign of the crew or further wreckage was found, nor was any sign of the motorized lifeboat or the dory. Investigators sent out calls to various ports to watch for the *Deering*'s crew on the supposition that some may have survived. A series of supposed sightings followed, all centering on the six Danish members of the crew. On March 20, a seaman certificate (No. 20,694) was issued in Portland, Oregon, to one Cyril A. McLellan. An investigation never found McLellan, however. All leads came up empty.

In June, the State Department forwarded requests for help to American consular officers in seaports around the world. The first request focused on the *Deering*. The second added another ship:

> Referring to the Department's confidential instruction of June 4, 1921, reporting the loss of the American schooner *Carroll A. Deering* under circumstances which are at least suspicious, you are informed that the American steamship *Hewitt* . . . disappeared on or about the same date and in about the same locality. There is nothing to connect the two casualties, except the similarity of date and place of occurrence. However, the Department is desirous of obtaining any information possible

regarding the present whereabouts of any member of the crew of either vessel in order to determine whether or not there has been foul play.

Pirates, it was now speculated, had attacked the *Deering* and the *Hewitt*, most likely killing the crews. The piracy theory grew to include other disappearing ships as well.

Evidence seemed to support it. A break had come April 11 when a local fisherman, Christopher Columbus Gray, found a bottle with a message on the beach just north of the cape. The message read, "*Deering* Captured by Oil Burning Boat Something Like Chaser taking Off everything Handcuffing Crew Crew hiding All over Ship no Chance to Make escape finder please notify head Qts of *Deering*."

By June, a team of three handwriting experts matched the note to papers written by *Deering* engineer Herbert Bates. Moreover, the paper was a type manufactured in Norway. The bottle was a type made in Brazil. It all fit.

On June 21, the *Portland Press* reported the handwriting results and laid out the growing story. The article was based in part on a statement from the preacher of Wormell's daughter, Lula, who had pushed for the federal investigation. The paper reported,

> The story of the inquiry, which has resulted in the conclusion that the *Deering*, the *Hewitt*, an oil steamer, which disappeared about the same time, and the *Cyclops*, which dropped unexplainably out of sight at an earlier date, may all have been victims of a pirate crew, was told to the *Portland Press* Monday evening by Rev. Addison B. Lorimer. . . .
>
> Needless to say it reads like a romance, and has all the salty tang and flavor of a story of the days of Capt. Kidd. Yet romantic and impossible as pirate theories appear to be in these modern days, the investigation documented by the allied departments to which reference has

been made seems to substantiate the belief that a torpedo boat chaser purchased from some foreign government at the close of the war by private individuals, has been out-fitted as a pirate craft and is preying upon vessels in the South Atlantic. Secretary of Commerce Hoover issued a statement yesterday regarding the fate of the *Deering* which bore out that conclusion.

Some speculated that Prohibition-era booze runners were involved. But the favorite theory in the press remained piracy. The Russian Revolution of 1917, which had brought Lenin's Bolsheviks to power, added an intriguing twist. To many, Russian pirates or their "red" sympathizers, who needed the kind of cargo hauled by the missing ships, seemed the most plausible pirates. Indeed, Hoover instruct-ed Richey to examine the ships' cargo lists for that reason. The navy continued to look in foreign ports for lost crew members and even other vessels.

Not all were convinced of nefarious goings-on. Captain William Merritt—the man who had left the *Deering*, sick, in Norfolk—told the *Bath Daily Times* in a story published June 23, 1921, that he wasn't buying it:

> "I am not convinced that pirates boarded the *Deer-ing*," said Captain Merritt today. "It has been my opinion from the first that the vessel went onto the rocks and that those aboard were swamped when they put off from the craft in small boats. Had the vessel been carried onto the beach it would have been an easy matter for all hands to have made shore by dropping from the jib-boom. That is the way I have felt since the word first came that the schooner was found on the rocks. The finding of the *Deering* as well as the reported disappearance of the *He-witt* at about the same time, came subsequent to the big storms when all craft encountered heavy winds as well as heavy seas, and I now feel that those aboard the two ves-sels have gone where they cannot be called."

Yet the Bates note remained. "That is the one mysterious touch attached to the whole incident," conceded Merritt, who had been Bates's superior. He had examined the note carefully himself. "I knew his writing, and its characteristics and for that reason I . . . believe that the note was written by him." Indeed, the writer had not only Bates's penmanship but also his peculiar habit of capitalizing words in the middle of sentences. "I am at a loss to account for anyone, not familiar with his way of writing, to fake a note such as this," the captain said.

By now, the disappearance of the *Deering*, the *Hewitt*, and their crews was worldwide news. The *New York Times* ran daily stories during the third week of June 1921. One on June 22 reported nine ship disappearances, using a four-deck headline: "MORE SHIPS ADDED TO MYSTERY LIST; Almost Simultaneous Disappearance Without a Trace Regarded as Significant. FOUL PLAY IN *DEERING* CASE; State Department Goes on Record as Suspecting It in the Fate of the Crew." The story began,

> The names of three other vessels which have disappeared . . . were added by the Department of Commerce today to the list of those whose failure to appear is attributed by the Government to circumstances more or less related to the supposed kidnapping of the crew of the American schooner *Carroll A. Deering* off Diamond Shoals, North Carolina, last January. It is not asserted that all the missing vessels were the victims of pirates or possibly Bolshevist sympathizers intending to dispose of ships and cargoes to the Government of Soviet Russia, but the fact that all these vessels disappeared at about the same time, and that none of them left a trace is considered significant.

The *Times* article reported the State Department's statement noting that the *Deering* had been seen on January 29 at the Cape Lookout Lightship and then, two days later, just a few miles north of that point "in such condition that there is every suspicion of foul play having occurred."

But was it really kidnapping?

In an accompanying Associated Press story, Maine senator Frederick Hale, who had called for an investigation at the urging of the captain's family, said he believed it was mutiny and not the work of pirates or Russians. "I think it will be found to be a plain case of mutiny in at least one of the cases," Hale said. "Possibly the mutinous crew of one vessel boarded the other to get a navigator."

The next day, the *New York Times* quoted the commissioner of navigation as saying, "I have heard many tall yarns of the sea but in this case the facts are there. The *Carroll A. Deering* and the *Hewitt* met some strange fate beyond that of ordinary vessels come to grief."

Theories were flying now. Piracy was still at the head of the list. Captain O. W. Parker of the United States Marine Shipping Board told the *New York Times*, "Piracy without a doubt still exists as it has since the days of the Phoenicians."

The more exotic version of the piracy theory—that involving Russians or Bolsheviks—was gaining currency on the national level. An FBI raid on the headquarters of a Communist front group in New York found papers that purportedly called on members to seize American ships and sail them to Russia. Indeed, some of the cargo on the missing ships was noted to be materials the Russians could not buy under an embargo against the new Communist regime. Stories began circulating that vessels with blacked-out names had been seen at Russian ports.

That was not the only possible explanation, however. One theory speculated that rumrunners out of the Bahamas had stolen the ship. The *Deering* was big enough to carry a million dollars' worth of Prohibition-era alcohol.

Mutiny still was a distinct possibility as well, particularly given the disagreements between the captain and his mate. That theory was given credence by the *Deering*'s passing the Cape Lookout Lightship with no officers aboard.

Of course, mutiny could have been followed by a pirate attack—or by the abandonment of the doomed ship and the drowning of the crew in their lifeboats.

Non-theories were flying, too.

A *New York Times* article on January 23, 1922, quoted both experts who believed in the pirate theory and those who thought that either a natural disaster had befallen the ship or that it had struck one of the many floating mines left over from World War I. Moreover, an accompanying story dismissed all talk of pirates. The article, datelined London, offered a perspective from experts on the other side of the Atlantic:

> All appearances, according to observers here, point to the abandonment of the *Deering* by the officers and crew when they saw that the vessel was foundering, or perhaps after she had run aground where she was found. That would account for the missing boats, which certainly would not be required by any pirates who boarded her and placed the crew in irons. They would naturally use those in which they arrived.
>
> What became of the crew of the *Carroll A. Deering* if they abandoned her? It is known that the steamer *Hewitt* . . . was in the neighborhood of Cape Hatteras, where the *Carroll A. Deering* foundered, at the time of the disasters. It is thought probable that the *Hewitt* was able to weather the rough sea for a time and picked up the crew of the schooner. When the *Hewitt* herself went down, all hands, including the crew of the schooner, would go with her.
>
> As to the theory of Bolshevist conspiracies to obtain a mercantile navy by piratical seizure, the probability is

that Bolsheviki would have taken the schooner rather than her crew and would have tried to save her cargo.

Still remaining was the matter of the note found on the beach. In August, that unraveled. An undercover federal agent began cozying up to the note's finder, Christopher Columbus Gray. Soon, the fisherman conceded he had written it himself. Gray initially escaped federal agents but was lured to the Cape Hatteras Lighthouse on the pretext of receiving a job for which he had applied. After his capture, Gray conceded he had faked the note—in hopes of gaining employment at the lighthouse.

The confession seemed to shoot down the theory of piracy. By September, many investigators concluded that most of the 10 ships that had disappeared in the Atlantic in recent months simply had fallen victim to the East Coast's most violent hurricane season in 22 years.

But a hurricane had not done in either the *Deering* or the *Hewitt*. What of them? Though Herbert Hoover believed the *Deering* had been boarded by outsiders, Lawrence Richey focused on the theory of mutiny. He came to believe the crew had taken over the ship and gotten rid of the captain, then been lost at sea themselves.

The theory of mutiny was plausible. It also was unprovable. In time, Richey and all the others gave up hope of learning the truth. Consular offices continued looking for the *Deering*'s crew members. But the investigation officially ended in 1922. No official finding was ever made.

The mystery continues.

Few artifacts remain to serve as clues. Some timbers that washed ashore on Hatteras after the *Deering*'s dynamiting were used to build Buxton homes in the 1920s. Part of the bow that floated down to Ocracoke remained there, visited by tourists, until Hurricane Ione returned it to Hatteras

The design of the Graveyard of the Atlantic Museum gives a hint as to what's inside: the capstan from the "ghostship" Carroll A. Deering, the "lost lens" of the Cape Hatteras Lighthouse, photos from Billy Mitchell's 1923 bombing tests, and numerous other artifacts related to the maritime history of the Outer Banks. Wilmington architect John Parker designed the building to look like a wrecked ship lying on its side, with timbers completing the ship's frame.

Photograph by Vicki McAllister

in 1955. A local gas station owner, Wheeler Ballance, collected the pieces and displayed them in front of his Texaco station in Hatteras Village until the early 1970s.

The most notable piece was the capstan, used to raise and lower the *Deering*'s anchors. It is now displayed at the Graveyard of the Atlantic Museum in Hatteras Village. So are some timbers and a boom from the *Deering*.

The schooner's disappearance is front and center at the museum. To this day, theories flourish. Pirates or Bolsheviks, mutiny or abandonment—all have their adherents. Paranormal explanations have gained traction as well. The ship's disappearance is sometimes tied to its location at the

The wreckage of the Deering, *including the distinctive capstan used to raise and lower the ship's anchors, has been a tourist attraction at several locations. After the disabled* Deering *was dynamited, the wreckage drifted to Ocracoke Island. There it remained until a 1955 hurricane brought it back to Hatteras, where it was displayed in front of a gas station. It now resides in the Graveyard of the Atlantic Museum.*

Postcard, author's collection

northern edge of the Bermuda Triangle.

But certainty has not been forthcoming. More questions than answers remain, as the museum postulates:

Did bad blood between the captain and his first mate lead to mutiny and a takeover? To murder?

Why was the captain's handwriting absent from the charts and maps after January 23?

Why had important papers been ransacked and taken?

Why had a meal been laid out—and abandoned?

Why did it take six days to sail the 90 miles from Cape Fear to Cape Lookout, a trip usually lasting no more than 12 hours?

Where were the officers when the ship passed Cape

Lookout? Were they being held below? Had first mate McLellan killed them?

If so, was it a case of murder or a full-blown mutiny of the ship? In other words, did McLellan operate virtually alone, or was the full crew part of the killing and/or take-over?

Was the tall, thin, red-headed man John Frederickson? He was the ship's bosun and the highest-ranking man aboard after the captain, first mate, and engineer. If McLellan were holding the captain and engineer at gunpoint below, it would have made sense for Frederickson to be in charge above.

Why were three pairs of boots, none of them Wormell's, found in the captain's cabin?

Where were the anchors?

What was the mystery ship that passed Cape Lookout but ignored the lightship's order to stop? Was it pirates? Booze runners? Why couldn't its name be seen? Was it intentionally covered? Was this the missing *Hewitt*? Could the *Hewitt* have been stolen by pirates, after which its new crew attacked the *Deering*?

Where were crew members when the ship finally ran aground? Where were their possessions? Had they simply abandoned the ship when they saw it would be smashed on the shoals at Hatteras? Had they already mutinied and taken over the ship? Had they already been kidnapped or killed by pirates or Bolsheviks?

The sea has never given up the answers. No one alive knows what occurred during the final days of the majestic sailing ship known as the *Carroll A. Deering*.

Its crew sails on, never at rest.

Chapter Five

WARS OFF THE SHORES

C arol White was nearly 13 years old and living on the island with her grandmother when World War II started. The red-headed tomboy grew up in a two-story home, cooked on a wood stove, and even had a water pump inside the house, a real luxury.

"Life was hard. We were all poor," Carol White Dillon says now, though she knows that mostly in retrospect. She had plenty to eat—pigs, seafood, oysters. Horses and cows ran wild on the island. "Life was very primitive back then," she says. "There was no crime then. The biggest crime was boys stealing watermelons."

Economic circumstances aside, life was idyllic. "When May 1st came, I was always allowed to take my shoes off," Dillon says. Riding her Ocracoke Island horse, Ivy, was her joy. "I'd jump on that horse, take hold of the mane, knee him, and away we'd go."

Life changed once the war started. It would make Carol Dillon famous under another name.

Remote Hatteras Island has been a magnet for war,

mostly because of its strategic location for shipping. Military action has come to its shores in five major wars: the American Revolution, the War of 1812, the Civil War, World War I, and World War II.

The number increases to six if you count the Civil War twice. Indecisive Hatteras came under attack from both sides.

Outer Bankers, especially those on Hatteras, were known for their ambivalence during the Civil War. Though North Carolina was part of the Confederacy, Hatteras was more inclined toward the Union. The federal government, after all, had been good to the Outer Banks, establishing forts and lighthouses. "Bankers could not have much sympathy with the revolt against a government which had been their constant friend," one Union officer wrote. Confederate troops considered the islanders opportunists for raising white flags on their roofs when either the Confederates or Yankees appeared.

One testament to the genuine division on the island was that the only two churches in Hatteras Village were both Methodist, at least until a 1937 merger. The Southern Methodist Church, nearer the northern end of the village, numbered among its faithful some Union sympathizers. The Northern Methodist Church, nearer the southern end, included some Confederate sympathizers. "My great-grandfather fought with the Yankees," one Hatteras Village resident remembered, "and he was a leader of the Southern Methodist Church. I always thought that was odd. Another great-grandfather that was captain of his own pilot boat, he sided with the South. He helped the blockade-runners through and everything."

Gibb Gray, an Avon man born in 1927, suggested during a park service interview that ambivalence was simply part of the island. His great-grandfather Evan Williams was a molasses trader and a navigator who became a sergeant stationed at Fort Hatteras. "I think he was Confederate," Gray said. "Here they didn't want to side with either one. . . . During the Revolutionary War, some people left here. . . . They didn't want to be in the revolution. They wanted to just stay with the British. They left here and went to the Caribbean, like the Bahamas, Jamaica and places like that."

But the Civil War came, whether islanders wanted it to or not. The Confederate army arrived on May 9, 1861, and immediately built two forts near Hatteras Village: Fort Hatteras on Hatteras Inlet and, less than a mile to the north, Fort Clark. The Confederate government commissioned privateers to use their own boats to capture Northern goods and vessels. A Union blockade was set up to stop the privateers, leading to the first naval engagement of the war, on July 21 at Oregon Inlet.

Full-blown warfare arrived shortly afterward. On the morning of August 28, 1861, the federal naval fleet began shelling the new Confederate forts in advance of an invasion. Landing barges deposited 315 troops, though high winds kept another 555 from coming ashore. After two days of bombardment and fighting, the Battle of Hatteras ended. Union forces took over both forts, sending Confederate soldiers to prison in New York.

That battle, the first Union victory of the war, is commemorated today by a state historical marker near the ferry landing at Hatteras Village: "Confederate Forts. Fort Hatteras and Fort Clark, 2 miles s. west, fell to Union troops on Aug. 29, 1861, after two days of heavy naval bombardment."

Within 10 days of the Union landing, nearly all male residents had sworn allegiance to the United States government. Still, locals did not necessarily fare well. Faced with

The Union captured Forts Hatteras and Clark at Hatteras Inlet after a two-day naval bombardment in August 1861, portrayed here in a Courier and Ives engraving. That began Union control of the island for most of the rest of the Civil War, though many islanders supported the North anyway.

Library of Congress

plundering by some federal troops, residents petitioned Union colonel Rush Hawkins: "Dear Sir: We, the citizens of Cape Hatteras, do ask of your honor that you will allow us to return to our homes and property and protect us in the same ways as natural citizens, as we have never taken up arms against your Government, nor has it been our wish to do so." Hawkins obliged, issuing orders that any Union soldier found plundering the locals was to be shot.

Hatteras was then fully under the auspices of the Union army. Moreover, anti-secessionists who had charged North Carolina leaders with treason for seceding now held their convention on the island. A provisional state government was set up there, too. Hatteras resident Charles Henry Foster was elected to Congress, though his election was immediately rejected by that body. A *New York Times* article put the legitimacy of this surrogate government in perspective: "The actual de facto jurisdiction of this Government is confined to the sand-bar recently captured by the U.S. Navy at Hatteras. The portion of this bar protected by the U.S. flag may be 15 or 20 miles long, by about one mile wide. Would it not be a hazardous experiment to reconstruct the political edifices on such a foundation?"

Federal forces occupied Hatteras during virtually the entire war, though the Confederates fought to get it back. In October 1861, they captured the tugboat *Fanny,* loaded with ammunition, winter coats, and supplies for a camp the Confederates did not know existed—Live Oak Camp in Chicamacomico, home to an Indiana regiment. The Confederates immediately plotted to capture the regiment, then use the camp as a steppingstone to proceed down the island to Cape Hatteras. There, they would blow up the redoubtable lighthouse.

That plan led, a few days later, to one of the more bizarre sequences of the war. Moving in small steamboats

America's 1st Attempt
at Civil War Reunification

Orchestrated by Union Col. Rush C. Hawkins,
the Hatteras Convention was held nearby on
Nov. 18, 1861. The state's secession was
declared null and void, Hatteras was
proclaimed the capitol and Marble Nash Taylor
became provisional governor. Taylor called for
a special Congressional election held Nov. 28
but, Charles Henry Foster's unanimous election
by the four island precincts was ignored
by the 37th U.S. Congress. Abraham Lincoln's
May 28, 1862 selection of Edward Stanley as
military governor effectively ended all claims
to any local government.

It may have seemed like the tail wagging the dog, but anti-secessionists charged the rest of North Carolina with treason and set up an ill-fated state government on the island. The New York Times, *noting this was only a "sand-bar," ridiculed the effort: "Would it not be a hazardous experiment to reconstruct the political edifices on such a foundation?" Nonetheless, an island monument standing today extols "America's 1st Attempt at Civil War Reunification."*

Photograph by Vicki McAllister

dubbed "the Mosquito Fleet," Confederates attacked the regiment from Pamlico Sound. Though unable to land, they chased the panicked Union troops, who took off running down the beach. The Northerners raced on foot southward to Cape Hatteras, accompanied by worried Chicamacomico residents. Confederate soldier E. C. Yellowly wrote in his diary, "The enemy saw [Captain Lynch and his troops] and began to run, leaving everything behind them, except their arms and accouterments. Our boys found Bibles, likenesses, papers and a great many things of like character." They ran for hours, the Confederates pursuing from the sound, periodically trying to get close enough to land. The nearly 15-mile run and the October heat caused many to drop in exhaustion.

Both groups rested overnight. The Confederates, bivouacked in the woods south of Kinnakeet, awoke the next morning to find that the Union ship *Monticello* had appeared and now was firing. This time, it was the Confederates' turn to run. They scurried aboard their vessels, moving quickly back north toward Roanoke Island.

The back-and-forth of October 5 and 6, 1861, came to be known as "the Chicamacomico Races."

Gibb Gray's great-great-great-grandfather Joshua Gray owned two large schooners that he kept anchored in the sound near Avon. Those schooners were caught up in the Chicamacomico Races, too, being fired upon by the Union. "They got fired onto from the ocean side because they did not know whether it was Confederate boats or not," Gray said in a park service interview. "They were fishing boats but they were big. One was the *Resolute*, and one was the *Worthington*." The damage was minimal, Gray said.

Winter storms and rough seas, not surprisingly, played a role in the war off Hatteras. A few months after the Chicamacomico Races, in January 1862, the ocean battered a

Union fleet of more than 100 ships trying to reach Fort Hatteras, delaying its arrival. Eventually, most of the ships made their way through Hatteras Inlet and up Pamlico Sound to bombard Confederate defenses on Roanoke Island.

More famously, a storm sank the ironclad USS *Monitor* on New Year's Eve in 1862. The previous March, the *Monitor*, dubbed "a cheesebox on a raft," had engaged in a legendary battle at Hampton Roads, Virginia, with the mighty CSS *Virginia*, better known by its former name, the USS *Merrimack*. That battle between the two ironclads, though indecisive, had ushered in a new era of naval warfare. No longer would wooden and sailing boats be able to compete with iron, steam-driven vessels.

The *Monitor*'s end came at the hands of not the Confederates but the Atlantic Ocean. Repaired and modified in October, the *Monitor* left Hampton Roads on December 29 en route to Beaufort, North Carolina. By the following night, a brutal storm overtook the proud vessel. The heavy waves caused a leak, and pumps could not keep up with the incoming deluge. "Finding the vessel filling rapidly with water," the captain later reported, "I ordered all the men left on board to leave the turret and endeavor to get into the two boats which were then approach[ing] us."

Four officers and 16 crew members were lost during the *Monitor*'s sinking, though another 49 were rescued by the *Rhode Island*. The corpses of five or six men washed ashore and were buried on the island. A state historical marker north of Buxton reads, "U.S.S. *Monitor*. Fought C.S.S. *Virginia* (*Merrimac*) in first battle of ironclad ships. Lost Dec. 31, 1862, in gale 17 miles southeast. First marine sanctuary."

The *Monitor* lay at the bottom of the sea for more than a century until it was discovered in 1973. Two years later, the site was designated America's first national marine

No ship could sink it, but a violent Hatteras storm did. "The Wreck of the Iron-clad Monitor," *a line engraving published in* Harper's Weekly, *shows the USS* Monitor *sinking on New Year's Eve 1862 off Cape Hatteras. The rescuing USS* Rhode Island *waits in the background.*

Harper's Weekly, 1863
U.S. Naval Historical Center

sanctuary to protect it from further deterioration and to allow government recovery of artifacts. The *Monitor*'s turret, steam engine, cannon, and more than 1,200 other artifacts are housed in the USS *Monitor* Center, which opened in 2007 at the Mariners' Museum in Newport News, Virginia.

Once the Civil War ended, life quickly returned to normal on Hatteras. Fewer than 100 slaves had lived on the island, so residents had little trouble adjusting to the new order. Economics were a more pressing concern. Linking themselves to the Union had cut off the islanders' trading opportunities with the Confederate mainland. Yankee soldiers, however, had bought Hatteras goods like fish and yaupon tea during the war. Now, Reconstruction brought the Union-supporting islanders steady jobs at the new lighthouses, lifesaving stations, weather stations, and post offices. In many ways, the Outer Banks fared better than the rest of the state.

Though the American public generally was not aware, and certainly did not know the seriousness of the intrusions, both world wars brought the Germans to the Hatteras coast.

During World War I, seven German submarines worked the waters of the East Coast. The U-boats blew up ships, killed crew members (though often allowing them to escape in lifeboats), stole or sunk cargo, and laid mines.

The German navy's newest, largest, and most modern submarine was the *U-140*. Dispatched in June 1918, it arrived in American waters that August. It had already sunk a 10,000-ton tanker the day before it reached the Hatteras area. Some 110 miles off Cape Hatteras, it sank the four-masted schooner *Stanley M. Seaman*, a 1,060-ton craft loaded with coal.

The next afternoon, the *U-140* found more prey, surfacing

within sight of the Diamond Shoals Lightship, 14 miles offshore. Its target was the coal-filled American steamship *Merak*. The steamer zigzagged down the coast, however, escaping the shells fired from the *U-140*.

Nearby, the lightship's first mate, Walter L. Barnett, heard the shelling and climbed the mast supporting the ship's light. He spotted the *U-140* with binoculars and fired off a wireless message to ships in the area: "Enemy submarine shelling unknown ship E.N.E. ¼ mile off lightship." A total of 31 ships received the message and were spared an encounter with the submarine.

The lightship itself was not so fortunate. Chased by the Germans, the *Merak* ran aground on Diamond Shoals. As the *Merak*'s 43 crew members escaped on two lifeboats, the German sub aimed at the lightship. "Her first shot took away our wireless," Barnett later told author David Stick, "but the next five were aimed wide and missed us."

Knowing it would not be long before the sub found the range again, Barnett got his crew off the lightship quickly. "Within ten minutes we had the whaleboat overboard, and the twelve of us had shoved off from No. 71," Barnett said, using the lightship's official nomenclature. "We had the seven oars, six fourteen-footers for rowing, and a sixteen-foot sweep oar. I put the large oar over the stern and six of the crew grabbed the others, and we headed to the west'ard as fast as they could row." The men rowed for five miles or so as the sub kept firing at their ship. Finally, they saw the lightship go down in the distance. The crew, using an oar as a mast, now put up sails. They finally saw land just before dark, a spot about a mile north of the Cape Hatteras wireless station. Barnett and the crew rowed down the coast and reported to navy headquarters.

Two days later, a United States destroyer damaged the *U-140* enough with depth charges that it had to return to

The Diamond Shoals Lightship, shown here in 1917, was a necessity for ships on the edge of the treacherous shoals. It paid for its helpfulness. In August 1918, the lightship's first mate radioed a warning of the presence of a German U-boat, saving 31 ships a possible encounter. The Germans intercepted the message as well, however, and after giving the crew time to abandon, sank the lightship.

U.S. Coast Guard

Germany. And six months later, a replacement lightship—No. 72, captained by Barnett—anchored off Diamond Shoals.

<hr>

As troublesome as U-boats were in World War I, it was during World War II, and particularly in the first six months of 1942, that the German presence off the Eastern Seaboard became devastating. Nearly 400 tankers, freighters, and even passenger ships were sunk by the submarines. Some 5,000 people were killed or disappeared.

Many of the losses came off Cape Hatteras, where the shipping lanes were especially important—and especially vulnerable. The events are noted on a state historical marker in Buxton: "Diamond Shoals. 'Graveyard of Atlantic.' German submarines sank over 100 ships here, 1941–42, in the 'Battle of Torpedo Junction.' Shoals are 3 mi. south."

The number varies—a more reliable count may be that 87 ships were sunk off the Outer Banks—but the dangers of the nearly catastrophic six-month war are not debated. Through it all, the American people knew very little, kept in the dark by censorship. That ignorance initially played into the enemy's hands. German U-boat commanders, intending to cripple United States and British shipping, did not even have adequate coastal maps. It didn't matter. They were surprised to find their way lighted by automobiles traveling along coastal roads.

"It was as if there was no war going on at all," Joseph Schwarzer, executive director of the Graveyard of the Atlantic Museum, said in a piece by author and filmmaker Kevin P. Duffus. "The Germans surfaced off the coast, and they marveled that they could sit there in their submarine and watch cars drive up and down the road, see streetlights, smell the pine forests in the breeze coming off the land. It was incredible."

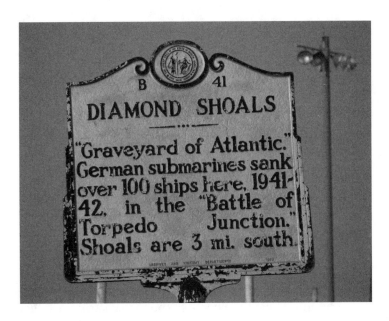

A state historical marker, its paint peeling, today is the most prominent reminder that World War II was fought off the North Carolina coast. German U-boats initially operated with little hindrance in the "Battle of Torpedo Junction." More than 80 ships, most of them tankers and cargo ships torpedoed off Cape Hatteras, were sunk in the first seven months of 1942 alone.

Photograph by Vicki McAllister

Schwarzer said one German crew member was asked later if he remembered Hatteras. "And he said, 'Remember Hatteras? Of course I remember Hatteras. It was remarkable. We would surface at night, we would see the lights on the beach, the targets would be silhouetted perfectly. The tankers would go by, we'd look at it. We'd say, "That one's too small. We really want a bigger target." ' I think most of the sub commanders could not believe their luck. That they were in an area where not only were the targets positively ubiquitous, but there was little danger of being attacked."

It made for easy pickings. On the first day of engagement,

January 18, 1942—just six weeks after Pearl Harbor—three ships were sunk off Cape Hatteras. The next day, another. The next day, another.

Islanders, despite the news blackout, couldn't help being aware.

Ignatius "I. D." Midgett of Waves turned 12 in 1942. "There [were] a lot of shipwrecks on the beach," he said during a park service interview. "During the war you could see them at night burning. You'd hear the explosions, whether it be torpedoes. And you could actually see the fires burning." He continued, "I never did see a body wash up, but lots of people did. There was a lot of wreckage that would wash up. There was actually a lot of oil on the beach back then where these tankers would be sunk off here and it would wash up on the beach. Big globs. If you went on the beach you wound up having to come home to use kerosene to get your feet clean."

As a boy, islander Gibb Gray heard the attacks of German U-boats on three United States ships, including the cargo vessel *City of Atlanta*. "I saw one big explosion in the middle of the night," Gray remembered. "It was about two o'clock and the house shook bad and my dad said, 'A ship's been hit.' I could see the red glow."

Gray also witnessed the attack on the oil tanker *Dixie Arrow*:

> On the way to school we saw all these bodies of young men. The school got lashed with another violent explosion. And looking down towards the lighthouse, we saw the smoke, the black smoke boiling up. That was the *Dixie Arrow*. We skipped school that day. We just didn't want to go that day. It was an exciting time that happened all of a sudden, with the war right at our doorstep. It was worse than Pearl Harbor. We ran up to Big Kinnakeet Station and we saw an airplane heading down that way,

The Dixie Arrow *tanker was steaming north on the night of March 26, 1942, approaching Diamond Shoals while carrying 96,000 barrels of Texas crude oil, when it was torpedoed by the U-71. Flames and smoke quickly overtook the tanker and rattled islanders as well. Eleven of the 33 crew members were killed, and the tanker sank. It could have been worse. Among the dead was a brave seaman, Oscar Chappell, who steered the burning tanker into the wind, saving fellow crew members but assuring he would be consumed by the flames.*

David Stick Collection, Outer Banks History Center

and about that time they were backing the lifeboats down into the water to go out and help.

Villagers eventually were required to blacken their headlights and keep their windows curtained, so as not to backlight American ships and continue giving the U-boats easy targets. "They had an army Jeep that ran through the community," one resident recalled. "If they saw a spark of light through the window, they'd rap on your door and tell you to shut it off."

Expanded Coast Guard patrols worked the beaches on foot, on horseback, and by Jeep, searching for spies. They sometimes found oil slicks so thick from tankers that they could not be broken up by the waves. Sometimes, the oil ensnared Jeeps in the sand.

It was against this backdrop that 13-year-old Carol White grew up.

"Things changed when the war started," Carol White Dillon says now. "We had to cover our windows. People painted their headlights with only a sliver showing. You were not allowed on the beach at night."

Ships were regularly attacked. "Everything in the world drifted ashore from the boats that were torpedoed—oranges, furniture." She once found "the beach loaded with automobile tires. This actually happened in the '40s. A Greek ship capsized, and all but one [man] died. He dug a hole on the beach to stay warm." She recalls hearing about a man's body washing up on the beach. Later, she learned that three men had been found dead in a bullet-riddled boat. The Germans, she was told, would strafe lifeboats with machine-gun fire.

Living in her home was her seventh-grade teacher, who, it turned out, was making mental notes on the tumultuous times. Fifteen years later, that teacher, Nell Wise Wechter, published a beloved children's novel on the 1942 war off

Hatteras. *Taffy of Torpedo Junction* featured the young, red-headed Taffy Willis—a fictionalized version of the real-life Carol White she knew so well.

Wechter's Taffy is an independent girl who rides the island on her pony and roasts crabs along the shore with her friends—and gets involved with a mysterious boarded-up shack. With the war on, she's warned to stay away from the beach. She doesn't, of course, and instead manages to capture a German spy who has come ashore.

"In real life, I didn't catch a spy," Dillon says. But fiction didn't fall too far from fact. "My mother did. My mother was a postmistress."

Maude White ran the post office in Buxton. She became suspicious when a local German man kept coming in to insure and mail large wooden boxes. "She called the FBI to open a suspicious box," Dillon says. Inside were "maps up and down the East Coast." The FBI followed the man, Hans Haas, to New York and arrested him for spying. Maude White got a commendation from President Franklin Roosevelt, Dillon says.

Much of *Taffy of Torpedo Junction* draws on the experiences of islanders, and specifically of Dillon. In the novel, explosions from ships rattle schoolroom windows, just as they often did for the real-life girl. In the book, too, Germans come ashore in a lifeboat. "In real life, we knew Germans were coming ashore in this manner," Dillon says. "We were not afraid because there was nothing on the island we thought they could damage. The radar, maybe."

Precocious Carol White, too, ignored warnings not to go to the beach. She and a cousin wanted to go swimming near the lighthouse on a moonlit night. "We were about to dive in," Dillon now says, when suddenly a voice demanded, "Halt! Who goes there?"

The cousin took off running. Carol stayed and turned

to see a Coast Guard patrolman confronting her with gun drawn. She feared her running cousin was about to be shot. He wasn't, but they both got a lecture they took to heart. "We really never went back to the beach after that," she says, laughing. From then on, they swam in Pamlico Sound.

The Battle of Torpedo Junction came to an end later in 1942. The Americans installed improved monitoring equipment, affording a better chance at finding U-boats. By May, American ships began traveling in convoys, as British vessels did. That, too, dissuaded German attacks. By July, four U-boats had been sunk. The Germans started pulling them out of United States waters.

Wechter's book appeared in 1957. *Taffy*, which a Raleigh newspaper columnist once called "perhaps the best piece of children's literature ever produced in the state," has been republished periodically. In the 2007–8 school year, it became required reading for North Carolina students. Wechter is deceased, but Dillon is in demand as a speaker for her story of the real-life Taffy.

Her non-Taffy story is a good one as well, representing one family's four-century saga on the island. "My people were shipwrecked here in the 1620s," she says of two Moeller brothers who sailed from Germany, and who changed their name to Miller upon arriving. One of the shipwrecked brothers moved to Tennessee. The other stayed on Hatteras, marrying a Native American woman named Mary.

Dillon's mother was the youngest of 13 children born to a descendant. "My grandfather fought in the Civil War," Dillon adds. For which side? "The wrong side, the Union," she says, laughing. "He didn't believe in slavery, so he would have fought for the Union anyway." But Christopher Columbus "Kit" Miller wasn't enamored of the North for long. "My grandfather became very embittered when Sher-

Carol White Dillon, here talking with visitors to the Chicamacomico Life-Saving Station, was a schoolgirl living on Hatteras during World War II. Her girlhood exploits became the basis for a beloved children's novel, Taffy of Torpedo Junction, *written by her teacher. Dillon, who operates the Outer Banks Motel in Buxton, is regularly called upon to talk about the book.*

Photograph by the author

man marched to the sea and burned all those homes."

After Dillon married, she and her husband opened the Outer Banks Motel in Buxton in 1955. She still operates what is one of the island's most popular motels. She lost her house and all her photographs to a fire in 1966 when power company workers sent a surge through the line. "Today, you'd sue," she says. "Back then, you just cried." Her daughter likewise lost her home to a fire in 2007.

But for all the interesting aspects of her life, Carol White Dillon is still best known for being the real-life tomboy whose wartime exploits became a part of North Carolina literature.

Shortly after she and her husband opened their motel, she had a chance to see the war from the other side.

"I had a guest in '56 or '57 who asked to use the typewriter," Carol White Dillon says. This was not just any guest. "He said, 'Ma'am, I was one of the U-boat captains that was torpedoing your ships.' He said, 'You know, Mrs. Dillon, we did not agree with what Hitler was doing. We did as we were told.' "

Chapter Six

THE LIGHTHOUSE

The summer day is comfortably warm, and tourists line up to buy tickets and take their turns. The 268 steps to the top are steeper than one might think, but how can one not climb the Cape Hatteras Lighthouse?

The country boasts few more recognizable symbols than Hatteras Light—with its black and white spiral stripes, standing atop a red-brick and granite base—nor few symbols more inspiring. The Statue of Liberty. The White House and the memorials in Washington, probably. What else? Mount Rushmore, perhaps. The arch in St. Louis, possibly.

The lighthouse, in other words, is on a very short list.

What the day's climbers are tackling is the second structure to be called the Cape Hatteras Lighthouse. This one is at its second location, moved at the end of the 20th century to avoid the approaching sea. The now-stabilized lighthouse is open for climbing from mid-spring through mid-fall. The double keepers' quarters are open year-round as a visitor center and museum.

Photographers line up, recording family members in front of the famous structure, as they have for generations. They shuffle side to side, back and forth, manipulating just the right angle, the tower dominating the frame from the background. They switch positions with their subjects, or ask a stranger to take the family portrait, so all will have proof they stood in the shadow of greatness.

Its imposing size is part of Hatteras Light's magic. At 208 feet or thereabouts, it is the nation's tallest brick lighthouse. Just as certainly, it is the most recognizable. Hatteras Light has been called one of America's three most important coastal icons, along with the Golden Gate Bridge and the Statue of Liberty.

The magic of this graceful structure is also tied to its history and its mission. For more than two centuries, a light has stood at the cape to warn sailors of danger. It has saved many from the Graveyard of the Atlantic.

The first documented shipwreck here was in 1585, and countless others followed. The shoals, winds, and currents at Hatteras formed a deadly conspiracy. Even when vessels attempted to handle them wisely, the Gulf Stream and southwest winds often proved too much. Unable to sail past Cape Hatteras, ships would tack back and forth at Kinnakeet (now Avon) until the winds changed, no matter how long that took. In 1904, naturalist H. H. Brimley went to the top of the lighthouse and subsequently wrote, "I counted twenty-one sailing vessels, all of them three and four mast schooners, beating back and forth unable to get around the point of the shoals. . . . [A] man connected with the life saving service told me that in August of the previous year, when the wind had remained southerly for twenty-six consecutive days, he counted no less than a hundred and five vessels weather-bound north of the Cape."

The combination of circumstances played havoc with

The spiral-striped Cape Hatteras Lighthouse, at 208 feet, is the nation's tallest lighthouse. It is also one of the most recognizable structures in the world. In summer, it hosts a steady stream of camera-clutching visitors.

Photograph by Vicki McAllister

America's young shipping industry in the 18th century. Various warning systems were tried. In the 1790s, in part with the backing of Secretary of the Treasury Alexander Hamilton—whom many credit with the "Graveyard of the Atlantic" appellation—the United States government authorized the first lighthouse.

That lighthouse was built in 1802–3. It must have seemed a truly impressive structure, a 90-foot octagonal sandstone tower that measured 120 fcct from its underground stone foundation to the dome roof. Inside the dome was a 10-foot-high oil lantern, to be filled with sperm whale oil carried to the top by lighthouse keeper Adam Gaskin.

It was not the only effort at Hatteras. So bad were the Diamond Shoals that the United States Lighthouse Service tried to put a secondary warning device out on them. Storms thwarted attempts to build a tower, however, so finally, in 1824, the Diamond Shoals Lightship was stationed on the shoals instead. Just three years later, a storm broke the ship apart. Not until 1897 did a second lightship drop anchor. That one stayed until being sunk by a German submarine in 1918. A third replaced it, remaining until 1967, when a tower structure finally was built.

The first lighthouse, meanwhile, never met expectations.

The light proved too low to be seen beyond the shoals—something that might better have been considered before the lighthouse was built. Moreover, ship captains complained about its dimness and low visibility. The beacon simply didn't penetrate the darkness beyond the shoals. As if that wasn't enough, storms often broke the windows and the lamp.

There wasn't much good to be said about Hatteras Light. One captain, in a fairly typical complaint, reported in 1837 that "as usual no light is to be seen from the lighthouse."

In 1851, a federal lighthouse board sought the views of

The little-remembered Hatteras Beacon Light was built in 1856 about a mile south of the lighthouse to offer a supplemental light. Shown here in 1893, the 43-foot-tall wooden structure was closed in 1898.

Photograph by U.S. Lighthouse Service
Outer Banks History Center

captains on lighthouses on the East Coast. Many were especially happy to give their views on Hatteras.

Lieutenant H. K. Davenport, skipper of a mail steamer, said, "Cape Hatteras light, upon the most dangerous point on our whole coast, is a very poor concern."

Captain C. R. Mumford one-upped him, calling Hatteras Light "a disgrace to our country."

David D. Porter, a former naval officer who then captained a coastal packet and who would become superintendent of the United States Naval Academy, trumped them both. He called Hatteras "the most important on our coast, and, without doubt, the *worst* light in the world." He continued, "The first nine trips I made I never saw Hatteras light at all, though frequently passing in sight of the breakers: and when I did see it, I could not tell it from a steamer's light, except that the steamer's lights are much brighter. It has improved much latterly, but is still a wretched light. It is all important that Hatteras should be provided with a *revolving* light of great intensity, and the light to be raised fifteen feet higher than at present."

Point made. Congress appropriated $15,000 to elevate the structure to 150 feet and to outfit it with a new Fresnel lens. Developed in France by Augustin Fresnel, the state-of-the-art lens used prisms and magnifying glasses to turn a small oil-wick flame into a powerful beacon. The new beacon revolved as well, thanks to a weight that slowly descended from the top of the tower to the base, engaging gears that turned the beacon. The descent took about 12 hours. The keeper then had to rewind the apparatus.

Work was completed in 1854. It seemed to have been worth the wait. A Buxton resident said the new light was "a beautiful lamp, made up of 24 beautiful prisms."

Just seven years later, however, it was out of commission. Confederates wanted to destroy the lighthouse to

The current lighthouse, shown here around the 1890s, was built in 1870 as a replacement. The original 1802–3 structure was enlarged and updated in 1854 after being called "without doubt, the worst light in the world." After the Civil War, it was still considered substandard. The second lighthouse has had no such complaints. Note the keepers' quarters to the far left.

Photograph by H. H. Bambeer,
U.S. Lighthouse Service,
Outer Banks History Center

deprive federal vessels of their guide. Though they failed in that effort, they did take the lens in 1861. The Union replaced it.

Problems with the dilapidated lighthouse were such that Congress planned a new one after the war. It would be 600 feet northeast of the old one—meaning some 1,600 feet from the Atlantic Ocean. It would also be much higher.

And it would be grand. The $150,000-plus replacement lighthouse included a foundation of yellow pine timber, topped by a granite foundation, then by granite and brick, then finally by the lighthouse itself. Some 1.25 million bricks were used. When completed, the lighthouse was 208 feet high and thus the tallest in the country.

The second Cape Hatteras Lighthouse was first illuminated on December 16, 1870, using a new lamp and Fresnel lens.

The light was upgraded to an incandescent oil vapor lamp in 1913 and then to an electric light in 1934. Further upgrades were made in 1950 and 1972. Electricity now rotates the beacon—which is actually two 1,000-watt lamps— and a photo cell turns it on and off. The rotating beam is visible for 20 miles in clear weather. Actually, it has been seen at sea from as far away as 51 miles.

One Buxton woman whose father was an assistant keeper lived in part of the keepers' quarters. "That little room upstairs, my sister and I had that for our bedroom," she said years later. "We'd take the screen out of the window nights and lay there and watch the rays. We used to have those old, lovely rays that go from the tower, the light. Just light everything up."

The Coast Guard took over lighthouses in 1939. Three keepers tended Hatteras, lighting the beacon half an hour before sunset and keeping it lit until dawn. That was often a chore. The Buxton woman recalled an especially stormy

The Fresnel lens installed in the first lighthouse when it was upgraded in 1854 now is on display in the Graveyard of the Atlantic Museum in Hatteras Village. The lens was once thought lost, but it had been removed by Confederates for safekeeping during the Civil War. Then it underwent 140 years of travel, theft, and vandalism, and even was reinstalled in the 1870 replacement lighthouse, according to historian and author Kevin P. Duffus. In 2002, the National Park Service agreed to lend the museum the bronze framework of the lens and all the prisms that had been recovered.

Photograph by Vicki McAllister

night. Her mother realized her father had forgotten his lantern and sent the daughter to deliver it. "She bundled me up and gave me the lantern and extra matches, and I had to almost bend double to walk against the wind," the woman recalled. "But I got up there, and he was so glad."

The keeper was responsible for not only the light, but for the lighthouse as well. When a hired painter walked

Two iconic Hatteras images have endured alongside each other for centuries: surf fishermen and the lighthouse. This photograph was taken about 1956.

Carolina Power and Light Photograph Collection, North Carolina State Archives

away from the job after spilling the wrong paint on one of the stripes, the woman remembered, the three keepers had to paint the famous black and white spirals. Her father led the effort. "I can see him now," she said. "They fixed this box, and they got on it from the top of the tower. They lowered him down. They kept lowering him till they got all that painted out. He had a cheering mob on the ground. We were all out there. He was a-whistling and carrying on himself."

Keepers had to see that the tower was painted every seven to 10 years. Painting the two black stripes and two white stripes, each going around the tower one and a half times, took up to four months. In 1939, a Civilian Conservation Corps crew took 194 man-days to complete the job. In 1995, a private contractor used 165 gallons of paint.

The lighthouse proved to have a role not only for ships but in the community, both as a point of pride and a gathering place. Picnics and horse races were often held near its base.

All was not fun and games. The forces of nature, as always, were at work. The lighthouse had been built nearly one-third of a mile from the sea in 1870. But those 1,600 feet were disappearing steadily, the sea gobbling up about 20 feet a year. By 1920, just 50 years after the light was built, the distance was 300 feet. Groins, dunes, rock, sandbags, and even synthetic seaweed were tried. None was a match for the ocean and winds.

By 1935, waves were lapping at the base. The lighthouse was temporarily replaced by a skeletal steel structure. By the late 1930s, however, natural forces and the beach control work by the Civilian Conservation Corps temporarily reversed the erosion. The light was returned to the 1870 tower.

But shoreline erosion returned. Though sandbags were used in the 1980s, the sea was only 120 feet away by 1987.

Moving the famed structure seemed one logical solution. In 1996, the National Park Service began seeking funding for a move.

The popular feeling on the island, however, seemed to favor keeping Hatteras Light right where it was, though perhaps with better protective measures. The feds feared it would fall into the ocean, but many others were not at all sure. A group called the Save the Cape Hatteras Lighthouse Committee contended the light was fragile, likely to crack or even topple during a move. "Save Not Move" bumper stickers began replacing the ubiquitous "Save Hatteras Light" stickers.

In 1998, legendary photographer and conservationist Hugh Morton added reasons of history and cost to the argument. "To turn tail and run by moving the lighthouse would tarnish its value as a monument to heroism," Morton wrote in the *Raleigh News & Observer*. He saw no sense in spending $12 million "to obtain a zebra-striped white elephant that would not be nearly as valuable to our state if it were moved."

Others had personal reasons for not wanting their landmark relocated. "It's not the same with it moved because it changed all my locations," a Buxton resident said. "I used to navigate by that out in the sound."

One Buxton resident got at another feeling many held: "People are fatalists here—that's why they were at terrible odds with the Park Service, that's why they did not want that lighthouse moved. It's an act of God; if God wants that lighthouse to move, you know, God'll move it. It was even deeper than that—now I'm speaking for them, OK? I'm dredging their heart for you. And nobody knows if I'm right or wrong. It was like, 'If you move the lighthouse, are you going to make us move next?' It was a real deep nerve."

Local governments and chambers of commerce sup-

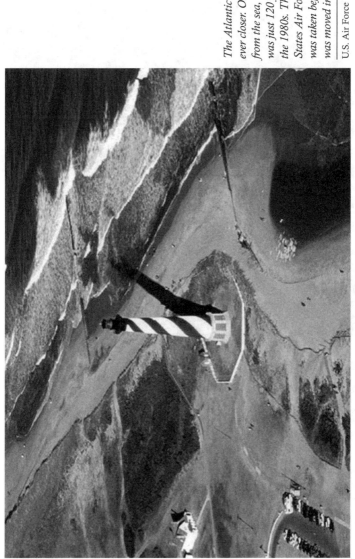

The Atlantic Ocean creeps ever closer. Once 1,600 feet from the sea, the lighthouse was just 120 feet away by the 1980s. This United States Air Force photograph was taken before the light was moved in 1999.

U.S. Air Force

It was called "the move of the century" in 1999 when Hatteras Light was pushed more than half a mile to the south-southwest. Roll beams were leap-frogged ahead of the lighthouse for each leg of the journey. "Watching the operation, you can't help but think of the pyramids," one woman wrote. The move took 23 days, capturing the attention of the nation.

Photograph by Barbara Rawes

ported keeping the lighthouse as it was and building more groins or erosion stabilizers—a solution opposed by environmentalists and the state. Dare County commissioners and private citizens went to court to block the move, to no avail.

Meanwhile, a report by North Carolina State University registered a dire note: "Move it soon—by spring 1999—or see it destroyed."

Congress decided to move the light, appropriating $12 million in 1998. A contract was awarded to the International Chimney Corporation of New York, which in turn contracted with Expert House Movers of Maryland and Virginia, as well as other subcontractors. They would move the lighthouse 2,900 feet—or slightly more than a half-mile—to the south-southwest, leaving it once again 1,600 feet from the sea. Outbuildings, including the keepers' quarters, also would be moved.

Work began in December 1998, and the beacon was extinguished in February 1999. The lighthouse was jacked up so that the 800-ton granite foundation could be moved. Crushed stone and steel mats were set up as a roadway. One hundred hydraulic jacks on rollers would slide the lighthouse along track beams.

On Thursday, June 17, 1999, at 3:05 P.M., Hatteras Light was given its first push. Ten thousand watched in a light rain. The first move was just four inches. After engineering checks, the lighthouse was moved another 10 feet that day, and 71 feet the next. Workers picked up the roll beams and the steel I-beam mat behind the lighthouse after the moves and laid them in front.

Often, crowds of more than 20,000 watched over the next three weeks. One spectator was Susanna Rodell, who visited with her daughter in late June and wrote the following for the *Raleigh News & Observer.*

What I was watching was a mammoth act of human will, a huge, unusual effort being made to save something solely because of its place in our emotions, in our collective history. It was, and is, an enormous act of love. All these humans, from the guys in hard hats driving the forklifts to the members of all the historical societies to the engineers to the Park Service folks, working their hearts out.

Watching the operation, you can't help thinking of the pyramids. It does the heart good to know that here in the late 20th century people are still willing to put all this collective wisdom and energy—not to mention millions of bucks—to work to save something that's really just a symbol, not religious, not political, just something tall and grand and old that has stood there all those years delivering the purest gift imaginable: light.

By July 9, the move was finished. The lighthouse was safe. Thousands cheered. Horns and sirens sounded. The move, expected to last four to six weeks, had taken 23 days.

On November 12, 1999, the beacon of the Cape Hatteras Lighthouse was relit during an extensive ceremony. Two singers offered original songs, William "Mojo" Collins performing "House of Light" and Beth Padgett singing "Hatteras, If a Lighthouse Could Speak."

The light already had a state historical marker alongside Highway 12 in Buxton. It noted, "Cape Hatteras Lighthouse. Tallest brick lighthouse in nation at 208 feet. Constructed, 1869–1870, to mark Diamond Shoals. Replaced 1802 structure."

Now, more awards were coming. The relocation of the lighthouse, declared "the move of the century," received the American Society of Civil Engineers' Outstanding Civil Engineering Achievement Award. The lighthouse, already on the National Register of Historic Places, was designated a National Civil Engineering Historic Landmark.

The lighthouse move is all the more remarkable when the distant new location is viewed from the vantage point of the old. The move covered 2,900 feet, and once again the lighthouse stood 1,600 feet from the sea.

Photograph by Vicki McAllister

Moreover, the Graveyard of the Atlantic Museum in Hatteras Village today exhibits a model of the original 1803 Cape Hatteras Lighthouse, which used oil lamps. It also displays the Fresnel lens installed in the lighthouse in 1854.

Hatteras Light remains the nation's tallest masonry lighthouse, though it is not quite its official height of 208 feet. The overall structure, including the foundation, has been measured at 207½ feet, of which about 10 feet are underground. The beacon itself is a little more than 192 feet above ground.

It is the very definition of an American lighthouse, the stuff of photographs and paintings, of poems and songs, and even of marketing plans short on imagination. Somehow, the graceful tower has come to be a salesman

The rotating beacon of the Cape Hatteras Lighthouse was designed to be seen at least 20 miles from any direction at sea. On land, from any angle, the lighthouse makes for a good photograph.

Photograph by Vicki McAllister

Hatteras Island

for everything from banks to saltwater taffy. It has been reproduced for snow globes, music boxes, beer steins, and even lawn decorations.

Excitement always attaches to the Cape Hatteras Lighthouse.

The climbers this summer day wait eagerly. Once the assault is under way, there is anticipation—and even apprehension—about the 268 steps of that tightly enclosed spiral staircase leading ever upward. Climbing Hatteras Light, after all, is not for those with breathing difficulties, let alone acrophobia or even claustrophobia. It seems remarkable that lighthouse keepers used to make this walk at least twice a day.

Youngsters bound up the steps this day, at least until fatigue momentarily slows them to a hurried walk. Here and there, climbers flatten against the wall to allow visitors to pass in the opposite direction. Some stop at the landings to look out or just to catch their breath.

As they near the top, everyone scurries up the final steps and out onto the landing.

Here, the view is majestic up and down the length of Hatteras Island, over to the mainland, out to sea. It is a time for smiles and excited chatter and, of course, family photographs. It is a time to rest and gaze a little longer, to reflect, to breathe.

There will be plenty of time to go back down.

Chapter Seven

HURRICANES

It was 1899, and S. L. Dosher was the United States Weather Bureau observer at Cape Hatteras, dedicated and trained well in his duties. But this was a hurricane the likes of which no one had ever seen, and he lived a mile from the weather station.

Dosher had waded home at eight in the morning in waist-deep water. Now, only two and a half hours later, he was trying to return to change the wind sheet.

Dosher got just one-third of the way. The water was now chest-high. He stopped at a neighbor's to rest. At noon, he started again, but the water was now shoulder-high. He had to wait until eight that night to leave, and even then, "I saw that the attempt was rash and fool-hardy and that I was certain to reach low places where I would be swept off my feet and drowned." The tide was the worst he had ever seen. So was the rain, which he described as "so thick and in such blinding sheets that it was impossible to see across a roadway 20 feet wide."

The hurricane of August 16–18, 1899—one of two to strike North Carolina that year—is sometimes referred to as San Ciriaco, named by the people of Puerto Rico after it killed hundreds there, on its way to a death toll of more than 3,400. It followed the warm waters of the Gulf Stream, slowed, and headed over North Carolina. The storm's entire right front quadrant fell over Hatteras and Ocracoke islands.

Even by Hatteras standards, this was an unimaginable storm.

Three days after its end, Dosher filed a report with Washington. The storm had begun as a 35- to 50-mile-an-hour gale on the morning of Wednesday, August 16, he wrote, and increased to hurricane strength early Thursday. At four that morning, it was blowing at 70 miles an hour. By ten, it had increased to 84. By one o'clock that afternoon, it was blowing at 93 miles an hour, with gusts from 120 to 140.

After that, the anemometer, or wind-measuring device, was lost. The winds grew greater from three o'clock to seven that night. Dosher estimated the sustained winds at over 100 miles an hour. They subsided for a half-hour during the night, then resumed at 60 to 70 miles an hour into the next morning.

More than a century later, Dosher's description of the great storm of 1899 is still chilling:

> The hurricane was, without any question, the most severe of any storm that has ever passed over this section within the memory of any person now living, and there are people here who can remember back for a period of over 75 years. I have made careful inquiry among the old inhabitants here, and they all agree, with one accord, that no storm like this has ever visited the island. Certain is it that no such storm has ever been recorded within the history of the Weather Bureau at this place.
>
> The scene here on the 17th was wild and terrifying

in the extreme. By 8 A.M. on that date the entire island was covered with water blown in from the sound, and by 11 A.M. all the land was covered to a depth of from 3 to ten feet. The tide swept over the island at a fearful rate carrying everything movable before it. There were not more than four houses on the island in which the tide did not rise to a depth of from one to four feet, and at least half of the people had to abandon their homes and property to the mercy of the wind and tide and seek the safety of their own lives with those who were fortunate enough to live on higher land.

Language is inadequate to express the conditions which prevailed all day on the 17th. The howling wind, the rushing and roaring tide and the awful sea which swept over the beach and thundered like a thousand pieces of artillery made a picture which was at once appalling and terrible and the like of which Dante's *Inferno* could scarcely equal. The frightened people were grouped sometimes 40 or 50 in one house, and at times one house would have to be abandoned and they would all have to wade almost beyond their depth in order to reach another. All day this gale, tide and sea continued with a fury and persistent energy that knew no abatement, and the strain on the minds of every one was something so frightful and dejecting that it cannot be expressed. In many houses families were huddled together in the upper portion of the building with the water several feet deep in the lower portion, not knowing what minute the house would either be blown down or swept away by the tide. . . .

Cattle, sheep, hogs and chickens were drowned by hundreds before the very eyes of the owners, who were powerless to render any assistance on account of the rushing tide. The fright of these poor animals was terrible to see, and their cries of terror when being surrounded by the water were pitiful in the extreme.

Dosher estimated the damage to Hatteras alone at $15,000 to $20,000, a whopping total in 1899 dollars. Fishing, the island's principal industry, he noted, "has for the present time been swept entirely out of existence." Both the island's single telephone line and its single telegraph line were down. Most homes were badly damaged, five or six so much that they were unfit for habitation. The Southern Methodist Church was destroyed. All bridges and footways were swept away. Roadways were piled from three to 10 feet high with wreckage.

Several vessels were wrecked or stranded. The Diamond Shoals Lightship had broken loose from its moorings and was a total loss. "A large steamship foundered about one mile off Hatteras beach . . . and it is thought all on board were drowned," Dosher added. No one on Hatteras died, though many nearly did. He noted that a pleasure boat at Ocracoke, immediately south of Hatteras, was lost and that some of the party aboard had drowned.

Dosher's report ended with a plea: "There has been no communication with this place by wire or mail since the storm, and it is not known when there will be. It is therefore requested that so much of this report as may be of interest to the public be given to the Associated Press for publication in the newspaper."

The storm was catastrophic. The annual report of the United States Life-Saving Service would note, matter-of-factly, the difficulties at stations up and down Hatteras Island:

Oregon Inlet station: "A camp containing five fishermen became separated from the main beach by an inlet which had been cut through" during the storm. "Surfmen managed to throw a heaving stick to the men, and, with a line, hauled them safely across the inlet." They took the fishermen to the station and gave them dry clothes provided by the Women's National Relief Association.

- Gull Shoal station, between what are now Salvo and Avon: "A body, which was identified as that of the cook of the wrecked schooner *Aaron Reppard*, was found on the beach and buried by the surfmen."

- Cape Hatteras station: "The houses of the keeper and a surfman were washed down, the station stables demolished, and the boathouse carried from its foundation." Several local families, driven from their homes, moved into the station until the storm subsided.

- Durants station, Hatteras Village: "Station patrol found the body of a man among some wreckage cast up by the sea. Found nothing to identify the wreckage except a plan with the name *Agnes*. . . . Surfmen gave the body decent burial."

Nine vessels were known to have wrecked off the coast during a 72-hour period, and another six were lost at sea without a trace, according to the Graveyard of the Atlantic Museum in Hatteras Village. Newspapers of the day concluded that at least 30 men died in the shipwrecks; the museum now says more than 50 lives were lost.

A few days after the storm, a Norfolk newspaper described the lower half of Hatteras Island's shore in stark terms: "The stretch of beach between Kinnakeet to Hatteras, a distance of about eighteen miles, bears evidence of the fury of the gale in the shape of spars, masts, and general wreckage of five schooners which were washed ashore and then broken up by the fierce waves, while now and again a body washes ashore to lend solemnity to the scene."

Hatteras Island is storm central in the United States, rivaling the Florida Keys as a hurricane magnet. Tom Carlson writes in *Hatteras Blues*, "Cape Hatteras is used by weathermen as a geographical point of reference for almost every eastern seaboard hurricane or storm regardless of whether or not it's tracking toward North Carolina. But it's equally true that for millennia North Carolina's outermost, thin rind of land has stuck its fragile chin out into the Atlantic and dared anything coming by to take its best shot. And many have."

They have indeed. National Weather Service records show that, for the past century or so, the state has experienced a major hurricane every two to three years. A good many have zeroed in on that fragile chin.

Historical accounts suggest that's nothing new. Though the 1899 storm remains among the island's most devastating, an earlier one was its most defining.

Hatteras got its current geography in September 1846. The designer was, appropriately enough, a hurricane. A huge storm, aided by continuous northeast winds, pushed a massive wall of water far inland, flooding the rivers and creeks of North Carolina's coastal area.

When the storm winds rotated, the water retreated over the Outer Banks, carving inlets as it went. On September 7, the water cut Hatteras Inlet. The next day, a second inlet was cut—to be named Oregon Inlet, for the first large boat to pass through it, the side-wheeler *Oregon*. Thus, Hatteras Island was given first its southern border and then its northern border, both by the same storm.

Redding R. Quidley experienced the 1846 hurricane, which he called "a heavy gale, a violent storm." Quidley was a pilot who worked Hatteras and Ocracoke and often walked between the two areas. He never thought they would be broken apart. Quidley said he was not alone in being astonished:

> The day the inlet was cut out, there were several families living where the inlet is now. . . . To their great

surprise, in the morning they saw the sea and sound connected together, and the live oaks washing up by the roots and tumbling into the ocean. I was well acquainted with the growth of the land where the inlet now is, I lived with my brother where the inlet is now. I have worked with him cutting wood and chopping yaupon, where now, I have no doubt there is three or four fathoms of water.

Five months later, the schooner *Asher C. Havens* became the first vessel to sail through the new Hatteras Inlet, where Quidley used to walk.

In the years before the weather service, storm tracking usually fell to lighthouse keepers and to the occasional pilot, like Quidley, who set his thoughts to paper. Lighthouse keepers couldn't always take measurements, however. In September 1876, a powerful hurricane called "the worst in many years" struck the area, but high winds disabled the recently installed anemometers at both Wilmington and Cape Hatteras, leaving no good record of the storm's top winds. Hatteras also suffered great damage in an August 1879 storm.

In 1880, the island's weather station moved from Buxton to Hatteras Village. (It would move back in 1957.) It was easy to see the difficulties of having the station directly on the cape. One meteorologist allowed as how "the climate of Cape Hatteras is fine but the weather is something to give a man ulcers."

The Hatteras Village station—now a weather museum and welcome center—was incorporated into the United States Weather Service when it was created in 1890. The station became intricately involved with the national hurricane-forecasting service upon its formation in 1898.

While the 1846 hurricane was the island's most defining, and the 1899 hurricane arguably its most destructive, 20th-century storms were not kind either. Newspaper accounts and Jay Barnes's definitive work, *North Carolina's Hurricane History*, document a number of the most destructive storms to hit Hatteras.

A late-season storm on November 13, 1904, reached Category 3 strength as it passed near Hatteras in the morning, bringing high tides and heavy rains. A September 1913 Category 1 hurricane sank several ships off the Carolina coast, including the schooner *George W. Wells*, wrecked 500 yards off Ocracoke. The 317-foot-long, 3,000-ton *Wells* was at the time the largest vessel of its kind in the world. The passengers and crew were saved by the men of the Hatteras Inlet Life-Saving Station during a 14-hour ordeal.

A 1933 storm devastated much of the island. One woman, a child at the time, remembered that it flooded Hatteras Village. Her father and uncle were away running a freight boat, so her mother and aunt gathered their children in one house:

> The tide came up. Mother and Aunt got the kerosene stove and put it on the dining room table to get it out of the water and cooked our meals. They were standing in water in the dining room, in water about to their waist, cooking food for the children! They were trying to keep us upstairs but we kids were wild with excitement. We'd never seen that before. . . . [After the storm] the whole island was covered with a slick, slimy clay from the mainland. . . . You couldn't walk without slipping. It was green.

The 1933 storm had a lasting impact. Afterward, the Civilian Conservation Corps set up camp near the lighthouse to build up the beach and establish a dune line that would affect the island in ways both good and bad from that day on. Wearing army uniforms, they cut brush from downed trees and piled it along the sand fences to trap sand on the beach. Avon resident Mason Meekins described the venture, looking back from the early 21st century: "They planted grass, built sand fences along the beach, and the blowing sand kept building up. When a dune would reach a height above the sand fence, they'd put another sand fence on top of that. Those are the hills that you see all along our coast today. The sand fences are way down below most of them. As the grass grew on top of them, blowing sand caught on the grass and the hills keep growing higher, thank the Lord."

A September 1936 Category 1 hurricane caused tidal damage and brought disease. Barnes writes,

> On Hatteras Island, residents once again had to reckon with the "hoigh toide on the sound soide." Rising water washed numerous homes off their foundations. Some families opened their doors to the storm, allowing floodwaters to wash through their houses, thus preventing the structures from being swept away. After the tides receded, brooms were used to sweep out the heavy silt that had collected on the floors and baseboards.
>
> The Hatteras residents were threatened by disease after the '36 hurricane, and drinking water was scarce. Large cisterns used to collect rainwater were contaminated after the storm, and each one had to be disinfected with bleach. . . . Until the cisterns could be cleaned and more rains could come, many of the people living on the island had no water to drink.

Hurricanes visit in late summer and early fall, but bad Hatteras storms can arise at any time of year. A freak blizzard in March 1937 blew a two-masted vessel, the *Duncan*, out of Pamlico Sound and onto the shore at Buxton. The O'Neal family was aboard at the time. L. P. O'Neal remembered years later the story he heard from his father, Captain Loran O'Neal: "My grandfather got Daddy up and said,

'Loran, you'd better come up here. There's something not right.' Daddy said he got up and you could hear a roaring. From the time he got shoes on, the boat lurched, broke the anchor chain, and broke the forward mast out of it. A blizzard! She went right across the southern reef . . . to Buxton. There wasn't nothing there then but a marsh. The bowsprit went right up . . . in the sand. My mother walked off of that."

A September 1944 hurricane, fueled by 100-plus-mile-an-hour winds, was called "the worst ever" by some on the Outer Banks. Its strong winds filled the sounds with ocean water, backing up rivers and creeks. A report from Hatteras Island said the winds blew the waters so far west that the sound was left dry for nearly a mile. When the hurricane's eye passed, the waters returned, flooding villages up and down the island.

In Avon, 96 of the 115 houses were washed off their foundations or otherwise severely damaged. Barnes writes of a dangerous irony created by the protective sand dunes built after the 1933 hurricane: "When the '44 hurricane's west winds pushed the sound into the village, the sand walls became a dike that prevented the waters from escaping. The massive surge could not continue on across the bank to the ocean, and Avon became a deep pool. Residents reported seeing cars and trucks completely covered by the tides. Houses drifted about, sometimes crashing into each other."

John Morgan, a newspaperman and public official who grew up during the Depression, was on college break in September 1944, visiting his grandparents in Hatteras, as were his aunt Mable and her son Earl. His grandfather and uncle were shrimping, waiting out the storm elsewhere.

That the hurricane was coming was no surprise, Morgan would write in his autobiography more than a half-century later. The radio had been crackling out warnings all day September 13 about the storm that would hit the next morning. Still, the intensity was shocking. "By 8:00 A.M., the wind was blowing at near hurricane force from the sou[th] east, bringing the sea tide over the beach, coming down the sand roads, and cutting under the house, on its way to meet the waters of the sound," Morgan writes. The sea tide cut deep furrows in the land. The sound tide inundated everything. The wind kept increasing. Morgan and his aunt began "shoring up doors and windows against the furious onslaught of the now huge waves coming in from the sound side and crashing up against the side of the house."

After an earlier hurricane, Morgan's grandfather had cut a six-inch hole in the corner of the living-room floor. Now, water was bubbling up through the hole. The back door was intentionally left open. The water soon was up to 18 inches inside the home—and still rising. An even worse potential intruder was the two-seater outdoor toilet situated 100 feet from the back porch. Morgan writes,

> Nana saw it coming—a huge wave tore it loose from over the pit, and it came barreling toward the house.
> "H'it's a-goin' to hit us!" shouted Nana.
> "Oh my Lord," moaned Mable.
> "Help, save me!" cried Little Earl.
> As fate would have it, the old toilet got snagged on two sturdy yaupons located just to the corner of the front porch, and it took a turn which carried it beyond the front porch and on its way toward the road in front of the house. It snagged on a fence post by the family graveyard, and after the tide went down it settled upside down in the road.

More trouble was on the way. A towering wave rolled across the marsh and hit the kitchen door so hard it was torn from its hinges. Morgan nailed a two-by-four across the door and nailed plywood over a window that had blown out. "We could feel a surge every time a wave would hit the house, thinking it would wash off the blocks at any minute. But the weight of the water which had been let in through the hole in the living room kept the house on its foundation." The cups blew off the anemometer at the weather station when the wind reached 85 miles an hour. Educated guesses were that it blew as hard as 125 to 130.

Meanwhile, ships were foundering, including one that littered the beach with tires and inner tubes. Several crewmen drowned during the storm, one resident remembered: "They had four, five of them stretched out in a Little Kinnakeet boathouse. . . . There was one of them they didn't find. They said he wandered off into the woods, and they found one of them later a few months after that in the woods. He wanted to go over there and die."

It wasn't just the recently dead whose bodies were scattered about. A graveyard was washed away, one Buxton resident remembered: "The skeletons was laying there with the buttons where they rotted off of the shirts. They dug them all up and took them down the road and buried them in another graveyard."

A few more recent storms have rivaled the hurricanes of 1899 and 1944, including the infamous Ash Wednesday Storm of March 1962. Swelled by a lunar tide, flooding from the nor'easter overtook the island, destroying homes and even opening an inlet north of Buxton. The inlet later was filled in.

Hurricane Gloria crossed the Outer Banks near Cape Hatteras on September 27, 1985. A Category 4 storm offshore but a Category 3 over land, it was touted as "the most powerful in years." But the lunar tide was receding, so devastating flooding was avoided. Only modest damage came to land, though some beach erosion was severe.

Hurricane Emily struck August 31, 1993. Many still remember the date. Hatteras was prepared, yet still the storm was devastating. Most had left the island in advance of the monster. Evacuations had been unpopular in the past, causing vacationers and merchants to suffer. But the devastation wrought elsewhere by Hurricane Hugo in 1989 and Hurricane Andrew in 1992 had been persuasive. So when officials on Hatteras and Ocracoke islands made the call 36 hours before Emily hit, few objected. Ocracoke ferries were filled, carrying cars to Hatteras. A steady stream of vehicles moved north on Highway 12 and off the island. An estimated 120,000 departed that portion of the Outer Banks. Only about 1,000 remained on Hatteras.

It was fortunate most were gone. Emily, a Category 3 hurricane, battered the villages of Hatteras, Frisco, Buxton, and Avon. Barnes describes the devastation:

> Gusting winds, unofficially clocked at more than 111 mph, snapped ninety-foot pine trees, toppled small buildings, and ripped away roofs. Six Coast Guard family homes in Buxton were leveled by what was at first believed to be a tornado. Later analysis showed that straight, sustained winds had caused the destruction. Mobile homes were rolled over by the blasts of wind, and others had their roofs peeled back "like cans of sardines." One resident watched as a telephone booth rolled off its foundation and into the street. . . .
>
> The flooding was made worse by the occurrence of a full moon, which brought even higher tides to the region. Cars were "floating" in several parking lots in Buxton. In numerous homes, waist-high waves broke through windows and rolled into living rooms. The flooding was about one to two feet higher than predicted on one-hundred-year flood maps, resulting in the need for revised maps for Hatteras Island.

Damage estimates were near $13 million for the 17-mile

stretch hardest hit by Emily. All told, about 700 buildings were destroyed or badly damaged. At least 25 percent of Frisco's residents were left homeless. A villager said she and her husband had built on family property they thought immune to flooding, until Emily proved otherwise. "We got wiped out just about," she said. "We had 42 trees down. It tore the back side of the house out. We sit here in the [porch] swing and watch the trees pop off."

No lives were lost on Hatteras, Barnes writes, but "Emily delivered the hardest blow to the banks of any hurricane in over thirty years. Businesses were devastated by the storm. . . . One popular sales item all along the Outer Banks was the now standard T-shirt that proclaimed 'I Survived Hurricane Emily.' Those who actually earned it by enduring the storm wore the message with pride."

The storms during the rest of the 20th century were not quite so devastating to Hatteras.

Strong west winds on the backside of Hurricane Bonnie in August 1998 brought significant sound-side flooding to the island. Gusts of 80 miles an hour were recorded at Frisco.

In 1985, Hurricane Gloria struck Hatteras and skipped out to sea, its powerful right front quadrant remaining over the ocean. Gloria still caused severe beach erosion, killing one person and causing $8 million in losses.

It was in 1999—a century after the island's first detailed catastrophic hurricane—that real damage came again to Hatteras. Hurricane Dennis was a Category 2 storm on August 30 but weakened and meandered off the Outer Banks for the next week. When it finally made landfall on Hatteras, it was as a tropical storm with winds of only 70 miles an hour, though gusts of about 100 were recorded up and down the coast, including 98 at Hatteras Village and 89 at Oregon Inlet. For the week, Ocracoke Island recorded a whopping 19 inches of rain. Residents reported the highest flooding since the September 1933 storm.

Here, Barnes describes the effect of Dennis on Hatteras, where phone lines were knocked down, severing communication between the north and south ends of the island:

> Just north of Buxton, an inlet was cut across the island, washing away a 3,000-foot section of Highway 12 near Canadian Hole, an area often prone to ocean overwash. A convoy of three N.C. National Guard vehicles discovered the breach on September 1 as Guard members attempted to deliver fuel, water, and food to nearly 5,000 people who failed to evacuate the isolated south end of the island. . . . The storm forced the postponement of the scheduled relighting ceremony at the Cape Hatteras Lighthouse, but the lighthouse weathered the storm without a problem, having been recently relocated to its new site farther away from the Atlantic. . . .
>
> Along the northern stretches of Hatteras Island, several vehicles were found buried in sand up to their door handles. Even a wrecker was abandoned by its driver after being caught in a deep drift. Beachfront erosion was heavy in Rodanthe, where waves washed over the swimming pool of an oceanfront motel and claimed at least five houses. These houses had already been condemned, but after the storm one resident described them as "physically missing." . . .
>
> "You just don't believe it," Debbie Bell told the *News and Observer* as she cleared lumber and debris from the front yard of her surf shop in Rodanthe. "Third row houses are now oceanfront. The first row is gone. There's always erosion. But how much there was, it's just unreal. I never expected to see that much."

Four years later, Mother Nature was at it again. Hurricane Isabel, which had been a Category 5 storm, diminished to Category 2 by the time it hit the Outer Banks on September 18, 2003, its winds measuring 105 miles an hour.

Hatteras Village was especially hard-hit by Isabel, as before and after pictures show. Motels and other buildings were ripped off their foundations and moved hundreds of yards by the flooding. Highway 12 essentially disappeared. Even after the waters receded, the village was cut off from the rest of the island by the formation of a new inlet. Filling the inlet and rebuilding the road took two months, during which time the only transportation was by boats and ferries.

Hatteras Island

Hurricane Isabel destroyed most of the Hatteras Island Resort in Rodanthe in 2003, as this sequence of photographs shows. The storm ripped the pier house from the fishing pier, then roared through the rest of the resort, ripping out the floor and ocean-side wall of the restaurant, lifting the roof off the 38-room motel, and destroying 31 of 36 cottages. The resort never reopened. The Rodanthe Pier itself, surprisingly, received minimal damage.

Photographs by T. J. Cary

That was more than enough. Isabel devastated the island's northern and southern populated areas, notably Rodanthe and Hatteras Village, though oddly sparing Avon in the middle.

Isabel's storm surge and flooding damaged thousands of houses on the Outer Banks. Horror stories of flooding abounded. Isabel's effect was similar to that of the island-defining hurricane of 1846 and the Ash Wednesday Storm of 1962: it established a new inlet. A 2,000-foot-wide "Isabel Inlet" now existed south of Frisco, effectively cutting Hatteras Village off from the rest of Hatteras Island. Automobile traffic on and off the island was by ferry until the road could be reconstructed two months later. Filling the breach cost $7.5 million, and rebuilding Highway 12 added another $3.5 million. Total damage on the island was estimated at $97 million, $72 million of it in Hatteras Village alone.

It is a life that Hatteras Islanders have come to know. Not by coincidence are the athletic teams at the island's combined middle and high school known as the Hurricanes.

Hurricanes, nor'easters, and bad storms generally are part of the price residents pay for their time on this island. John Morgan, writing of the 1944 hurricane at his grandparents' home, puts it aptly: "Hatterasmen were accustomed to these storms. Although there were many broken windows and doors, missing shingles, a missing out-house, and considerable water damage, there was nothing insurmountable that could not be repaired. . . . A well-known characteristic of Outer Bankers is that they always stick together during hard times, and with everyone pitching in and helping, things were soon set back in place and order restored."

That is an enduring assessment. On Hatteras, people are accustomed—or as accustomed as they can be—to the brutal storms that come with what seems to outsiders alarming frequency. They have shown through the years that they will persevere. Generation after generation, they have proven that.

Likely they will be given the opportunity to prove it for generations to come.

Chapter Eight

MUSIC IN THE AIR

Reginald Aubrey Fessenden was arrogant, abrasive, and condescending. He was underfunded, lacking in public-relations skills, a poor businessman—and his name has been largely lost to history.

He was also a genius.

Fessenden began showing his aptitude in the 1880s and 1890s. In his early 20s, he moved to New York and went to work for Thomas Edison's laboratories, where he rose to the position of chief chemist. At Edison's behest, he invented an insulated coating for electrical wires that helped correct overheating that started fires within plaster walls.

Moving to George Westinghouse's laboratories, Fessenden next designed a light bulb that was superior to Edison's. There seemed little he couldn't do. Stephen Kirk, in his book on those other early-20th-century inventors on the Outer Banks, *First in Flight: The Wright Brothers in North Carolina*, notes,

> The ease and offhandedness with which Fessenden came up with some of his inventions is remarkable. One day, finding that the piles of paper on his desk were becoming unmanageable, he invented microphotography.

Another time, frustrated that he had to leave his offices to call for workers scattered far and wide over the research complex, he invented the pager. The holder of more than five hundred patents over the course of his career, he invented such things as the electric gyrocompass and silicon steel. He held an American patent on what his supporters say was a workable television system in 1919, but lacked the funds to develop it. It wasn't until seven years later that television came into being in England.

Fessenden was often far ahead of the times. One of his first patents was for a parking garage with ramps and hoists. The patent expired long before anybody needed parking garages.

After Westinghouse, Fessenden worked as an electronics professor for Purdue University and what would become the University of Pittsburgh. At these stops, he pursued his passion for radio, which he called "wireless telephony." His work, however, was always in the shadow of the better financed Nobel Prize winner Guglielmo Marconi. Marconi had sent wireless messages in dots and dashes in 1895 and gained worldwide fame in 1901 for transmitting a wireless telegraphic signal across the Atlantic Ocean. But Fessenden's theory of continuous-wave transmission would prove superior to Marconi's belief that electrical waves were transmitted in sharp blasts of energy. Indeed, in Fessenden's 1932 obituary in the *New York Times*, the head of General Electric's main laboratories described him as "the greatest wireless inventor of the age—greater than Marconi."

By the end of the 19th century, the United States Weather Bureau was impressed enough to hire Fessenden. He quickly proved it a wise decision. In 1900, Fessenden transmitted startlingly clear Morse code messages for the bureau. Two months later, he transmitted by wireless the first intelligible human speech—his own, asking an assistant, "One, two, three, four. Is it snowing where you are, Mr. Thiessen?" The historic transmission went a mile between two United States Weather Bureau towers in Maryland.

The bureau funded a larger operation for him on the North Carolina coast. Its need for quick, reliable weather information, especially during storms, was obvious. The telegraph line that ran down the Outer Banks was often knocked out of commission. Likewise, the cable traveling under Pamlico Sound to the mainland was at the whim of the elements, subject to currents, shoals, and corrosion.

Wireless seemed a promising alternative. Fessenden began his program in January 1901. He moved to Manteo for 20 months of experiments, establishing his main facility at Weir Point on Roanoke Island. Fessenden hired staff for that facility and others at Cape Hatteras and Cape Henry, Virginia.

It was a time of innovation on the Outer Banks. Just six miles from Fessenden's Roanoke Island site, the Wright brothers were at work perfecting flight. Helen Fessenden later wrote in her biography of her husband, "It was a companionable thought that in this element, the air, two men not so many miles away from us were achieving mastery in one form while we at Manteo were achieving mastery in another."

Fessenden's breakthrough was in early 1902, when he became the first to transmit musical notes, sent from his Kings Point tower at Cape Hatteras and received at his 50-foot tower on the northern end of Roanoke Island.

His achievement seemed to open wider opportunities.

On April 3, 1902, Fessenden wrote from Manteo to his patent attorney: "I have more good news for you. You remember I telephoned about a mile in 1900—but thought it would take too much power to telephone across the Atlantic. Well, I can now telephone as far as I can telegraph, which is

At Cape Hatteras in early 1902, Reginald Fessenden became the first to transmit musical notes by radio, which he called "wireless telephony." "I have sent varying musical notes from Hatteras and received them [on Roanoke Island] with but 3 watts of energy," proclaimed Fessenden, shown here in an undated portrait, "and they were very loud and plain, i.e., as loud as in an ordinary telephone."

General Negative Collection, North Carolina State Archives

across the Pacific Ocean if desired. I have sent varying musical notes from Hatteras and received them here with but 3 watts of energy, and they were very loud and plain, i.e., as loud as in an ordinary telephone."

Word of the discovery was heard loud and plain. The *Elizabeth City North Carolinian* reported on July 10, 1902, "Wireless telephone communication is a fact. Instruments invented by Professor R. A. Fessenden have been installed in homes along the coast, near Cape Hatteras and Roanoke Island and for a distance of 14 miles the ticks from the wireless telephone instruments can be heard over the telephone."

Trouble lay ahead, however. Fessenden rebuffed the effort of the head of the United States Weather Bureau, Willis Moore, to be listed as co-owner of his various wireless patents. Moore responded with staff cuts and threats that the bureau would begin using Marconi's rival radio system. Fessenden complained to President Teddy Roosevelt, but his letter ended up in the hands of Moore, who cut Fessenden's staff still further and recommended his firing. Fessenden instead resigned in September 1902. It was part of a nearly lifelong pattern of Fessenden and his employers being at odds over the ownership of patents.

Now, Guglielmo Marconi is most often credited with inventing radio, and Fessenden's singular achievements are little more than footnotes.

Coincidentally, Marconi visited Hatteras in 1904, just two years after Fessenden broadcast his musical notes. Marconi arrived on the island to inspect the 157-foot-tall tower constructed by the Marconi Wireless Telegraph Company, staying aboard a yacht anchored in Pamlico Sound. The tower, near Cape Point, was the first in Marconi's network. Soon afterward, it became the first commercial wireless station in the Western Hemisphere. Demand for

Fessenden stands before his rival Guglielmo Marconi's tower in Buxton. Two years after Fessenden's transmission, Marconi was on the island, inspecting the tower for his new Marconi Wireless Telegraph Company. Today, Marconi is often credited with inventing radio, while Fessenden's achievements have become a historical footnote.

David Stick Collection, Outer Banks History Center

"marconigrams" was so intense that the station operated 24 hours a day.

In 1912, the weather station in nearby Hatteras Village received one of history's most important telegrams—though it could do nothing to stop one of the world's great disasters. Richard Dailey, the 21-year-old grandson of Captain Benjamin Dailey, the first winner of the Congressional Medal of Honor for lifesaving on the Outer Banks, was the supervisor the night the station received a startling distress call from a sinking ship. The ship was the HMS *Titanic* on its maiden voyage more than 2,000 miles away in the North Atlantic. It had struck an iceberg in the cold waters off Newfoundland. The first the world knew of the disaster was the telegraph signal received on little Hatteras Island. Dailey reduced the signal to writing and relayed it to Norfolk on his ground-line telegraph instrument.

Or so one version has it. The story is told in different ways, and with numerous twists.

Island historian and tour operator Danny Couch says that, until his death in 1967, Dailey not only contended that Hatteras received the first distress call from the *Titanic* but that word was relayed to New York, where David Sarnoff was on duty. Sarnoff, who later founded RCA, is often cited as having received the first signal from the ship. But according to Couch, Dailey said Sarnoff didn't believe the *Titanic* had gone down.

Couch interviewed Dailey's widow, Dina, in 1976. " 'My husband was working the wireless . . . with Horace Gaskins,' " he says she told him. After Dailey got the SOS, he forwarded it— and paid a price. " 'He was reprimanded for junking up the lines.' " Dailey maintained that, had he been listened to, hundreds of lives could have been saved.

Another version adds that, later that fateful night, Dailey picked up a message from the *Carinthia* (probably the

SS *Carpathia*, the ship that rescued *Titanic* survivors) that it was going to the aid of the sinking ship. Already rebuked, Dailey refrained from passing on that message.

Meanwhile, Reginald Fessenden, though rarely gaining wealth from his inventions, became the first to make a two-way wireless transmission across the Atlantic (in January 1906) and the first to send voice across the ocean (in November 1906). He also made the first radio broadcast in history, a 1906 Christmas Eve program from Massachusetts that consisted of his short introductory speech, a phonograph recording of Handel's *Largo*, Fessenden's own violin solo of "O Holy Night," a prayer, and a wish of Merry Christmas. The program was heard at least as far south as Norfolk, Virginia. Radio operators at sea were astonished to hear human voices and music over their sets.

The 1912 *Titanic* disaster impacted Fessenden in another way, Kirk writes. Shortly after the ship's sinking, at a train station in Boston, Fessenden bumped into an old friend who worked for the Submarine Signal Company. The friend asked if radio waves might be used to communicate between submarines. Could they also help locate icebergs? "A new door open to him, Fessenden went back to serious work," Kirk writes, "eventually producing a pair of noteworthy breakthroughs: the sonic depth-finder, or fathometer, and elementary sonar."

There is little by which to remember Fessenden now, even on Hatteras. His tall wooden tower was knocked over by a hurricane in 1916. It was replaced with masts from a wrecked schooner, then replaced again with steel towers in the early 1920s. Three decades later, they were removed.

Buxton has built a community center bearing his name, however, and a historical marker stands near the northern entrance to the village. Another was placed on Roanoke Island. The marker at Buxton reads, "Radio Milestone.

From near here in 1902, R. A. Fessenden sent the first musical notes ever relayed by radio waves. Received 48 miles north."

That is only technically true. Fessenden's achievement, it turned out, was received around the world.

Chapter Nine

THE LIFESAVING
STATIONS

Most days, the lookout had little to do. Scanning the ocean, hour by hour, was tedious. Few people were about, even in summer. Only the relentless wind and waves were in evidence most days. Sea gulls might fly by or gather on the beach. Perhaps once a day—sometimes more frequently, sometimes less—a ship or steamer would venture up or down the coast. For the most part, the lookout had little to report.

The late afternoon of Friday, August 16, 1918, proved different. The lookout of the Chicamacomico Coast Guard Station—a facility transitioned from the Chicamacomico Life-Saving Station just three years earlier upon the birth of the United States Coast Guard—saw a steamer heading north. It was perhaps seven miles off the coast. Suddenly, a great mass of water shot into the air, covering the rear of the steamship. An explosion had rocked the ship. Smoke began pouring out. The steamer continued north, but only for a moment. Then it swung around and headed to the beach.

The Chicamacomico Life-Saving Station, restored as a museum and educational complex, is the nation's most complete example of a late-19th-century station. The building pictured here is the 1911 replacement station, which houses the visitor center, museum, and gift shop.

Photograph by Vicki McAllister

The lookout quickly reported to the station keeper, John Allen Midgett, Jr. The time was 4:30. Cap'n Johnny Midgett gathered all available hands. They headed out into the rough surf in a recently retrofitted naphtha-powered surfboat.

"The fire was now seen to shoot up from the stern of the steamer and heavy explosions were heard," Midgett reported afterward in the station's logbook. Surfboat No. 1046 would become famous, but for now, it was overmatched. The seas were moderately heavy, Midgett said, the winds from the northeast. The breakers were more than the surfboat could overcome. Cap'n Johnny and his five men had trouble even clearing the beach. It was not until five o'clock that they managed to get away. A half-hour had been lost.

Five miles offshore, they ran into a lifeboat. Aboard were the boat's captain and 16 men. "I was informed that their ship was a British tank steamer, the *Mirlo*, and that she was torpedoed which caused the fire, explosion and loss of ship," Midgett's report said matter-of-factly.

The attack came as World War I was nearing an end. In time, it was discovered that the steamer actually had struck a mine laid by a German submarine. The effect was the same. The *Mirlo* had been carrying a full cargo of gasoline—some accounts say high-octane aviation fuel—loaded in New Orleans and destined for England. The steamer was ripped apart. The fuel leaked.

The sea now, literally, was on fire.

Two other *Mirlo* lifeboats had been launched, but one had capsized, the captain said. He feared the remainder of the crew of 52 had died in the burning waters.

What followed remains one of the most amazing stories in the history of the North Carolina coast—as well as in the history of the Coast Guard and the history of maritime rescues everywhere. What followed was too implausible for any book or movie. What followed could not have happened.

Nonetheless, it did.

~

The Chicamacomico Life-Saving Station sits just inside Rodanthe, the northernmost village on Hatteras. It has been restored as a museum and educational complex, the nation's most complete example of a late-19th-century life-saving station. A must-see for tourists, it offers interpretive programs about rescues and the lives of surfmen.

It is surprisingly easy to envision the station's surroundings of a century ago, especially for visitors who have just driven through the nearly barren national seashore. It is easy to envision the surf, winds, and storms. It is easy even to envision the isolation.

The demanding work of the surfmen, however, is harder to grasp. Their duties now seem the stuff of legend. And yet ample evidence, both anecdotal and historically documented, exists. Indeed, United States Life-Saving Service regulations seemed to expect nothing less. A station keeper was required to attempt every rescue, no matter how difficult, trying every technique until the rescue proved impossible.

Patrick Etheridge, keeper of the Cape Hatteras Life-Saving Station, once uttered what became an unofficial motto of the service and, subsequently, the Coast Guard. Clarence P. Brady, the lookout who spied the legendary "ghostship" *Carroll A. Deering*, related the story in a 1954 issue of *Coast Guard* magazine: "A ship was stranded off Cape Hatteras on the Diamond Shoals and one of the Life-Saving crew reported the fact that this ship had run ashore on the dangerous shoals. The old skipper gave the command to man the life boat and one of the men shouted out that we might make it out to the wreck but we would never make it back. Etheridge

The distinctive 1874 lifesaving station, seen from the newer building, is in the center of the photograph. Immediately to the left, partially obscured, is a building once used by the surfmen for cooking and bathing. Farther left is a 1907 house originally owned by Cornelius Payne Midgett, brother of famed keeper John Allen Midgett, Jr. It is open to the public today. Two modern homes are in the upper right. Note the water that can pool throughout the complex after Hatteras storms, which come frequently.

Photograph by Vicki McAllister

The 1911 station sometime after it became a Coast Guard facility.
Chicamacomico served as a United States Life-Saving Service station from 1874
until 1915, when the service was transitioned into the United States
Coast Guard. The station was retired in 1954.

Aycock Brown Collection,
Outer Banks History Center

looked around and said, 'The Blue Book says we've got to go out and it doesn't say a damn thing about having to come back.' "

The importance of commercial shipping in the 19th century required the creation of first the United States Lighthouse Service and then the United States Life-Saving Service, officially begun in 1848. By the next decade, a few facilities were located on the Carolina coast.

It was not until the 1870s, however, that a dependable service was built. The Chicamacomico Life-Saving Station was established at Rodanthe in 1874 during a building blitz. Seven stations were authorized on the North Carolina coast that year, including three on Hatteras.

The 1874 Chicamacomico station was typical of the style of the time. A two-story, 20-by-44-foot structure served as watchtower, record room, and sleeping quarters. The six surfmen who slept in one small room upstairs received $40 per month and $3 per shipwreck during their December-through-March duty. They manned the watchtower during daylight and took shifts walking the beach at night and on low-visibility days. Their supervisor, the year-round station keeper, was paid $200 a year.

Some 188 people died in shipwrecks during the winter of 1877–78 within a 30-mile stretch of the Outer Banks, including crewmen aboard the USS *Huron*, which foundered off Nags Head in late November near a lifesaving station that had not yet opened for the season. It was time to step up the lifesaving efforts. Congress authorized 11 more stations, including five on what is now Hatteras Island. At the same time, it added a seventh surfman to each keeper's crew. It also extended the season to run from September to April.

A total of 29 lifesaving stations eventually were built in North Carolina, most of them in the 1870s and most on the

During the winter of 1877–78, an astonishing 188 people died in shipwrecks in a 30-mile stretch off the Outer Banks. A newspaper lampooned the situation with this cartoon, captioned "Death on Economy" and quoting Uncle Sam: "I suppose I must spend a little on Life-saving Service, Life-Boat Stations, Life-Boats, Surf-Boats, etc.; but it is too bad to be obliged to waste so much money." Congress quickly authorized 11 more stations, including five on what is now Hatteras Island. It also added to crew sizes and extended working months.

Harper's Weekly, December 29, 1877,
Library of Congress Prints and Photographs Division

Outer Banks. What is now Hatteras Island had 10 stations at—north to south—Oregon Inlet, Pea Island, New Inlet, Chicamacomico, Gull Shoal, Little Kinnakeet, Big Kinnakeet, Cape Hatteras, Creeds Hill, and Durants.

The stations were six or seven miles apart, with halfway houses in between. A surfman on "beach check" would walk to the house, exchange tokens with a counterpart from a neighboring station to confirm the trip, then return. Given the nature of Hatteras weather, the tokens were a necessity. Even a fundamentally honest surfman might be inclined to cut short the trip during a nor'easter.

As the lifesaving stations took hold, the number of shipwreck victims declined. Surfmen grew to enjoy a special status similar to that of the lighthouse keeper at Cape Hatteras and the men who served on lightships. Their jobs were coveted and often figured into local politics. Surfmen, after all, were among the few on the Outer Banks who held steady jobs. They gained an off-island "worldliness" as the Life-Saving Service periodically rotated them and their families to other locations. Moreover, their stations provided various services to travelers and emergency communications and medical assistance to the locals.

Each of the stations had its own stories of heroism, but the Pea Island Life-Saving Station boasts a unique history. Pea Island, separate from Hatteras until a 1945 inlet closing, is now best known for the eight-mile-long Pea Island National Wildlife Refuge, a major stopover for migratory birds along the Atlantic Flyway. The lifesaving station was erected in 1878. Following the elevation of a black man to keeper in 1880, Pea Island became the only station ever manned by an all-African-American crew.

Richard Etheridge, recommended by a Revenue Cutter Service officer as "one of the best surfmen on this part of the coast of North Carolina," was the Pea Island keeper. His appointment, under the prejudices of the day, allowed him to supervise only African-Americans. The appointment must not have been altogether popular. Shortly after it was made, the station burned down. Etheridge supervised its rebuilding and instituted rigorous lifesaving drills that made his men "one of the tautest crews on the Carolina Coast," in the words of one observer.

Sixteen years later, the Pea Island men would need all their skills. A three-masted schooner, the *E. S. Newman*, caught in a severe October 1896 storm that would become a hurricane, drifted nearly 100 miles to the Outer Banks before grounding two miles south of the station. Aboard were not only the captain and crew but the captain's wife and

In 1880, Pea Island became the nation's first—and only—station manned entirely by African-Americans. The crew, headed by keeper Richard Etheridge (left), is shown here in 1896. That year, Etheridge's men famously saved 10 people from the E. S. Newman, including the captain's wife and son, during a hurricane. They were honored for the deed 100 years later.

U.S. Coast Guard

their three-year-old son.

Etheridge had suspended patrols during the hurricane. But a watchman in the lookout tower, scanning the storm-darkened evening sky, thought he saw a red flare in the distance. He lighted a signal in response and notified Etheridge. A red torchlight from the *Newman* confirmed the watchman's find.

Helping seemed impossible in the storm. Etheridge got the Pea Island crew together anyway, hitching a pair of mules to the apparatus cart and heading down the beach. "The storm was raging fearfully," he later reported. "The storm tide was sweeping across the beach, and the team was often brought to a standstill by the sweeping current." Though they finally reached a spot opposite the ship, the men had no dry land from which to fire their cannonlike Lyle gun with its lifesaving line. Etheridge instead tied two of his strongest surfmen together on a line, had them take hold of another line, and sent them into the breakers. It was a dangerous and desperate move. Though the seas exhausted the two men, they returned with a crewman from the ship. Substitutes were needed for the two lifesavers, then substitutes for the substitutes. But each alternating pair managed to return with another of the nine aboard, including the child.

The prejudices of the day precluded the Pea Island lifesavers from being honored as white crewmen would have been. Gold lifesaving medals finally were awarded posthumously a century later.

The Pea Island crew's heroism was typical of that displayed up and down the coast.

John Midgett and his crew of the Cape Hatteras Life-Saving Station also were awarded gold lifesaving medals, for rescuing nine souls from the *Ephraim Williams* three days before Christmas 1884. Joined by the keeper of the Creeds

Hill station, they launched a lifeboat through a bruising surf to reach the ship.

The investigating officer wrote words that applied to other surfmen as well: "These poor, plain men, dwellers upon the lonely sands of Hatteras, took their lives in their hands, and, at the most imminent risk, crossed the most tumultuous sea that any boat within the memory of living men had ever attempted on that bleak coast, and for what? That others might live to see homes and friends."

Most of the lifesaving stations are now distant memories. About half still stand as private homes, businesses, or restored facilities. The station at Little Kinnakeet, just north of Avon, has recently undergone refurbishing. Plans are in place for the Oregon Inlet station at the island's northern end as well.

Chicamacomico is the crown jewel. The complex contains the original 1874 structure, which was converted to a boathouse after a larger station was built in 1911. The 1874 structure now houses the famed Surfboat No. 1046. The site also showcases the 1911 station, now a visitor center and museum.

Linda Molloy, Chicamacomico's operations manager, says the 1874 station was built on the ocean's edge, which in hindsight may not have been the best spot. "Storms moved it three times in the first four years," she says. It was relocated about 1911 when it became a boathouse. Finally, in the 1980s, it was moved to the current location.

Given the dangerous work, one Chicamacomico statistic is particularly noteworthy. "They never lost a life here in the line of duty," Molloy says. "Pneumonia was the number-one cause of death overall at lifesaving stations."

Molloy talks about the Midgett family, whose history is intertwined with the station. Some details are unclear. The

The abandoned, storm-battered Oregon Inlet Life-Saving Station (above) *stands sentry on the northern coast of Hatteras Island, along Oregon Inlet. Renovations to this facility are planned as well. Meanwhile, the Little Kinnakeet station north of Avon, already has undergone renovation.*

Photographs by Vicki McAllister

Most of the island's small lifesaving/Coast Guard stations were closed last century, their work consolidated at larger facilities. This Coast Guard station stands on Hatteras Inlet near the Graveyard of the Atlantic Museum and the dock for the ferry to Ocracoke Island.

Photograph by Vicki McAllister

Midyett family originated in France, she says. Matthew Midyett and his wife sailed to the Pennsylvania-Delaware area in the 1700s. They later moved to the Outer Banks either to try a new area or to avoid a legal dispute, she says. They settled near where the Bodie Island Lighthouse is today. Matthew had seven or nine male children, who moved to Chicamacomico, receiving sound-to-ocean parcels of land.

Records show that Matthew, who died in 1734, did indeed receive 1,900 acres on Bodie Island in 1722. But family legend says he washed ashore in the early 1700s after his ship wrecked during a hurricane. He married a local woman and had eight children with her.

Regardless of the precise details, the Midgetts—some

family branches spelled the name Midgette—had a profound influence on Hatteras Island, especially the Chicamacomico area. "Old-timers called this 'Midgett Town,' " Molloy notes.

When the federal government began protecting the coast, the Midgetts were obvious candidates for employment. "They were the first people to be offered light-keeping jobs because they knew the waters," Molloy says.

The first keeper, or officer in charge, at the Chicamacomico Life-Saving Station was Benjamin Pugh in 1874. Bannister Midgett III took over in 1879, starting a long run of official lifesaving Midgetts on the island.

No local hero was bigger than Rasmus Midgett, awarded the Gold Lifesaving Medal of Honor for rescuing 10 people off the shipwrecked *Priscilla*—all by himself. Midgett was patrolling on horseback about three in the morning after the disastrous hurricane of August 1899, during which 13 ships were wrecked. He came across the *Priscilla* just off the beach.

Having no time to alert the station, Midgett swam to the wreck and called to the crew, "Next time, one man—jump! I'll take care of you! One man. Only one!" One by one, seven men jumped into the sea, and Midgett carried them through the pounding surf to safety. Three were still aboard, too weakened to jump. Midgett climbed lines that hung from the ravaged rigging, found a crew member, and carried him to safety. Twice more, he repeated the procedure. It has been called the greatest solo water rescue in history.

The Midgetts are merely the best known of the island's lifesaving families. Many on Hatteras sought employment in the Life-Saving Service. As one observer put it, "If you look at the rosters of the lifesaving stations, you can tell where the station is by the names. . . . A mixture of Grays, Meekins, and Scarboroughs are in Avon; then a few Davises thrown in, you know you're in Buxton. You get to Hatteras, you're going to see some Ballances, Styrons, Burrus."

And Chicamacomico?

"Midgetts, Midgetts, Midgetts is Chicamacomico."

Midgetts today know the heritage. Fisherman C. E. Midgett heard the family stories while growing up, he says. He owns a copy of Nell Wise Wechter's book *The Mighty Midgetts of Chicamacomico*, but his is missing a few pages. He has been searching for years for a complete book.

C. E. Midgett didn't enter the lifesaving business himself. He was born in 1950, just four years before the Chicamacomico station closed. Still, it is part of his life. "My great-grandfather Clarence E. Midgett got the gold [lifesaving award] for the *Mirlo* rescue," he says proudly.

Ten Midgetts have won that award—given for lifesaving at extreme peril to one's own life—over the years. The Midgetts, it seems, collect lifesaving awards the way others collect baseball cards.

⁓

Cap'n Johnny Midgett assessed the scene quickly. The *Mirlo* was ablaze. Its captain believed one lifeboat had capsized. He feared most of the 52 crew members were dead in the burning waters.

Midgett, keeper of the Chicamacomico station, told the *Mirlo*'s captain to head toward the beach with his men. They shouldn't try to land, he warned, since the wind and waves were building to dangerous levels. They should wait for him to return. Without assistance, the men would be capsized.

Now, what would Midgett do?

The keeper didn't know the details of what he faced. It was the summer of 1918, and the Germans had been attacking shipping lanes along the East Coast. Indeed, the *U-117*

Chicamacomico's 1914 crew in Surfboat No. 1046, which would become famous four years later.

Chicamacomico
Life-Saving Station and
Museum

had laid mines from New England down to Rodanthe. The submarine's final nine mines had been placed right here, along Wimble Shoals, just two days earlier. The *U-117* was gone now—two days later, it would sink a Norwegian ship off Cape Hatteras—but the mines were as effective as torpedoes.

The *Mirlo* had made it safely from New Orleans, even passing Cape Hatteras without the assistance of the Diamond Shoals Lightship, which had been sunk by the *U-140* on August 6. But then one explosion, and then another, had nearly ripped the *Mirlo* apart. The tanker's captain briefly steered north before heading for the beach. After the second explosion, he ordered his men into two lifeboats and a small captain's launch. One boat capsized, throwing 16 men into the sea. They were able to grab the capsized boat, but only for a moment.

A third explosion ripped the ship in half, spewing gasoline over the water. David Stick, in *Graveyard of the Atlantic*, recounts the next moments:

> One boat, the Captain's, was soon clear of the sea of fire; the second, without oars, drifted aimlessly before the wind which was steadily increasing in velocity; while the third, the one that had capsized, remained near the sinking vessel, in the very path of the burning fuel still gushing from her hold. The men clinging to her sides were themselves covered with gasoline, their clothes and their hair and even their bodies on fire. Only by remaining under water for as long as breath would hold out, then coming up again for a hurried breath of air and submerging once more, where they able to remain alive; even so, in short order ten of them disappeared from view, leaving only six still holding on to the overturned boat.

Cap'n Johnny and five men of the Chicamacomico Life-Saving Station moved toward the sinking *Mirlo* in Surfboat No. 1046.

On July 23, 1930, Captain Johnny Midgett and five others of the 1918 Chicamacomico crew made history. They were awarded the exceedingly rare Grand Cross of the American Cross of Honor by Rear Admiral Frederick C. Billard.

Chicamacomico Life-Saving Station and Museum

They faced a wall of fire. The fuel had turned the ocean into an inferno. Flames shot as high as 100 feet into the air. Acres of the sea were ablaze.

"On arrival I found the sea a mass of wreckage and burning gas and oil," Midgett later reported. "There were two great masses of flames . . . in places covered with the burning gas."

Midgett steered the boat toward a crack in the flames. The surfmen grabbed their oars. Barely able to see, they maneuvered the surfboat between what at times were great sheets of fire, all the while fighting thick black smoke.

The surfboat's paint was scorched by the flames and heat. Its wood blistered.

But the men saw what they were looking for. "In between the two great flames at times when the smoke would clear away a little," Midgett reported, "a life boat could be seen bottom up[,] six men clinging to it, the heavy swell washing over the boat."

The six remaining *Mirlo* crewmen were exhausted and singed by fire—and disbelieving. They had given themselves up for dead. Only the rising wind and waves had saved them temporarily from the fire. Now, suddenly, a surfboat of saviors appeared.

The Chicamacomico surfboat pulled the six aboard. The crew then navigated back through the flames to the open sea. Midgett and company circled the inferno but found no signs of the missing lifeboat. The captain's boat, already headed back toward the shore, carried 17 men. The capsized boat had held these six, not including the 10 who died. But the missing launch, the smallest of the three, had carried 17. Where was it?

Finally, at dusk, Midgett and company found the missing boat drifting helplessly in the thick smoke. The men aboard were blackened and nude. When their boat caught

They couldn't have done it without the boat. Surfboat No. 1046, scorched and blistered by flames, stayed afloat during the famed Mirlo rescue. It sits now in the 1911 station behind the Chicamacomico visitor center.

Photograph by Vicki McAllister

fire, they had taken off first their shirts and then the rest of their clothing to beat out the flames. Still, their lifeboat—and their flesh—had been burned.

Surfboat No. 1046 towed the charred lifeboat toward shore, meeting up with the waiting *Mirlo* captain's lifeboat. Leaving both boats there, it carried the first group of survivors ashore. The waves were higher than ever. As other lifesavers on shore shined powerful lights on the breakers, the surfboat headed out a second time—then a third, then a fourth—to the waiting lifeboats. It was nine o'clock that night before the surfboat landed safely with its final group. The marathon effort had taken nearly four and a half hours. But all 42 survivors had been rescued.

The lifesavers—Johnny Midgett, Zion S. Midgett, A. V. Midgett, Prochorus L. O'Neal, Leroy S. Midgett (who was also the watchman), and Clarence E. Midgett—received public acclaim and the United States Gold Life-Saving Medal of Honor. Thanks came from both sides of the Atlantic. Great Britain gave the six its King George Medal for Bravery. The British Board of Trade issued Cap'n Johnny an engraved silver loving cup, now displayed at the station.

A state historical marker was erected near the Chicamacomico entrance for the brave men of the *Mirlo* rescue. Over the years, stories have been written and songs sung. Their heroic tale has been told for generations.

And then there was this. Some 12 years after the rescue, in 1930, the Chicamacomico lifesavers received the highest award of the United States government: the Grand Cross of the American Cross of Honor, an award initiated in 1906.

Only 11 people have ever won the Grand Cross.

Six of them rode together that night in Surfboat No. 1046.

Chapter Ten

FIREPOWER
IN THE AIR

The small airport in Frisco with a 3,000-foot runway is surrounded by a chain-link fence. The gate
is open. Half a dozen planes sit at attention. Sand
dunes and sea gulls are the only other spectators in the area
this day.

Billy Mitchell Airport has been open to the public since
1960. The National Park Service owns the land, but the
state's airport division operates this site, used primarily by
small turboprop planes and light business jets. The island
strip is by far the smaller of two named for Mitchell; the
other is General Mitchell International Airport in Milwaukee. The Frisco strip is on a remote 100 acres near the Atlantic Ocean, a mere 17 feet above sea level. It closes at night.
It has no lights. It has no fuel. It has no staff.

Somehow, you get the feeling Billy Mitchell would have
been fine with all that, as long as it involved airplanes.

The wind sweeps from the sea across the runway and
the plane tie-down area. Off to the side is a small covered
pavilion out of the rain and wind. A case includes a small
display entitled, "Mitchell Demonstrates Air Power."

Indeed he did.

Two airports are named for Mitchell, including General Mitchell International Airport in Milwaukee, which has 42 passenger gates. The other is this small strip in Frisco, Billy Mitchell Airport. It has no gates, save the one for the outside fence.

Photograph by Vicki McAllister

Brigadier General Billy Mitchell was a World War I aviation hero. Afterward, while stationed at Langley Field in Virginia, he visited Hatteras for its waterfowl hunting. He went back often, Molly Perkins Harrison writes in her book, *It Happened on the Outer Banks*:

> Always wearing knee-high cavalry boots around the village, Mitchell was a frequent visitor. . . . He dined with a local family, stood in duck blinds on Pamlico Sound, and fished out of Hatteras Inlet. One memorable photograph shows him on the porch of a Hatteras cottage with a bag of ducks, while another shows him on the docks next to a huge yellow-fin tuna. Aviation made it easy for Mitchell to make a quick escape to Hatteras, landing his De Havilland on the hardest patch of sand he could find. Though it was nearly two decades after the Wright broth-

ers' first flight, Mitchell's plane was probably the first airplane many of the Hatteras Islanders had ever seen.

Mitchell had led nearly 1,500 American and Allied aircraft in the Saint-Mihiel offensive in France in 1918. That made him history's first joint-force air commander. And a star.

Not surprisingly, the general was a keen proponent of air power. Mitchell said it would prove essential in modern warfare. As he put it, "Air power, both from a military and an economic standpoint, will not only dominate the land but the sea as well." He set about persuading the nation's political and military leaders, a task more difficult than one might imagine today—and that doesn't take into account Mitchell's personality. Like Reginald Fessenden, Mitchell could be arrogant. Unlike Fessenden, he was adept at going public with complaints against superiors. John T. Correll, former editor in chief of *Air Force Magazine*, wrote an article that described Mitchell this way:

> He was already a celebrity. Newspapers followed what he said and did. He was awarded the Croix de Guerre by the French. In England, Mitchell had an audience with King George V, and he took the Prince of Wales up for an airplane ride.
>
> Mitchell believed that the world stood on the threshold of an "aeronautical era" and that military airpower should be independent of ground and sea forces. He was inspired by the example of the Royal Air Force, established in 1918 as a separate service, combining the air arms of the army and navy.
>
> The irrepressible Mitchell constantly cast aspersions at his superiors, whose enthusiasm for airpower (and for Mitchell) was strictly limited. En route home, Mitchell told his fellow passengers on the Cunard liner *Aquitania* that "the General Staff knows as much about the air as a

hog does about skating." His comment was reported in the newspapers, of course.

Mitchell's biggest roadblock was a formidable one. General John J. Pershing, famed commander of the American armies during World War I and general of the armies afterward, believed air power should be subordinate to infantry. After the war, he made sure his like-thinking West Point classmate, Major General Charles T. Menoher, was appointed to head the air service—this despite Menoher's being an artillery officer who had never flown. Mitchell was named Menoher's assistant, a slight that seemed to have little dissuasive power.

"It was not in Mitchell's makeup or temperament to be deferential or to support policies he disagreed with," Correll wrote. "He worked around Menoher from the start, and behaved as if he were the Chief of Air Service. Menoher, who could not match Mitchell in publicity or support in Congress, gritted his teeth."

Mitchell made few strides, however. He believed "changes in military systems come about only through the pressure of public opinion or disaster in war." After all, British public opinion, responding to bombing by German zeppelins, had been responsible for the creation of that nation's air ministry. Mitchell hoped American public opinion would succeed as well.

To gain it, he needed to prove that air power was superior to sea power, particularly in guarding the coast—a navy responsibility—and while functioning under a shrunken postwar military budget.

Some naval officials already supported the use of air power. Admiral William S. Benson, the chief of naval operations, however, said simply, "I cannot conceive of any use that the fleet will ever have for aircraft. . . . The Navy

Brigadier General Billy Mitchell was no friend of his superiors when he showed them up with a memorable air power demonstration off Cape Hatteras in 1923. But he was always welcome among the islanders.

U.S. Air Force

doesn't need airplanes. Aviation is just a lot of noise." Benson disbanded the Navy Aviation Division but did not inform Assistant Secretary of the Navy Franklin D. Roosevelt, who denied before Congress that the division was defunct. Mitchell produced a copy of Benson's directive.

Meanwhile, Mitchell told the *New York Herald* in 1919 that the air service should be separated from the army as an equal branch—and a superior branch to the navy. "The air will prevail over the water in a very short space of time," he said.

The following year, he told Congress air power could sink any vessel, then set about to prove it. The navy, failing in its attempt to have Mitchell fired, instead beat him to the punch with a limited bombing demonstration. Even that demonstration was successful. But the navy downplayed and even mischaracterized its own results.

Facing pressure from Congress, the navy agreed to a limited demonstration by Mitchell. In 1921, off the Virginia coast, he conducted a series of bombing raids on three captured German warships in June and July and on the obsolete USS *Alabama* battleship in September. All four ships were sunk.

The most significant of the vessels was the German battleship *Ostfriesland*, built to be unsinkable. The *New York Times*, reporting from the assembly area the night before the two-day demonstration, said, "Naval officers are insisting that the fliers will never sink the *Ostfriesland* at all."

Pershing, the secretary of war, the secretary of the navy, 18 members of Congress, various admirals and generals, and 50 news reporters watched the proceedings from a transport ship. Despite numerous restrictions on their bomb dropping, Mitchell's flyers sank the unsinkable battleship.

The public understood what had happened, though army and navy official reports, signed by Pershing, minimized the success. Mitchell wrote his own report for Menoher, who filed it away. Nonetheless, some of Mitchell's report wound up in the *New York Times*. "Had the Army Air Service been permitted to attack as it desired," Mitchell wrote, "none of the seacraft attacked would have lasted 10 minutes in a serviceable condition."

Some still were not convinced. So in 1923, Mitchell was back, this time off remote Hatteras Island, and operating under stricter requirements set up by the military.

First, he had a makeshift landing strip built by locals near Hatteras Village, as proof that it could be done without great difficulty. He went to Ander Austin's family store in Hatteras to enlist local men for the hurry-up job. They built the temporary ocean-side airstrip using shovels, hoes, and horse-drawn carts.

One recruit was the store owner's six-year-old son, Shank Austin, who years later told how the general paid him a man's wages for hauling buckets of sand on the back of his pony. All the workers labored alongside a tractor pulling a weighted pallet as they filled holes, tidal pools, and marshy areas, then packed level the landing strip.

Meanwhile, Mitchell brought in about 30 airmen from Langley Field. They struggled with the Hatteras elements, eventually moving into the Durants Coast Guard Station.

Ben Dixon MacNeill, in *The Hatterasman*, tells his version of "Billie" Mitchell's place in the islanders' affection:

> And then on a day in August, 1923, Billie Mitchell again flew in. It was not ducking season, nor goosing season, and he never seemed to care much about mere fishing. He had other things on his mind and these things he communicated to everybody. He hired men and horses and carts, and when Shanklin Austin, aged six, presented himself and his horse for employment, Billie Mitchell hired him right off. He was to haul sand from the beach

and fill up some holes on the flats. Shank got three dollars a day for himself and the stocky little native horse got three dollars. The cart seems to have been for free.

Nobody doubted that Billie Mitchell could do and would do what he proposed to do. He would sit on the counter of Shank's father's store of an evening and tell about it. When they got the holes filled up there would be a lot more aircraft, big ones with two engines, which could carry bombs weighing as much as a thousand pounds. There were going to be two battleships tethered to their anchors, or maybe turned loose with their engines going, and Billie Mitchell was going to drop these bombs down their smokestacks and cause them to sink.

It was as simple as that and nobody doubted that he could do it and would do it. When the holes were filled up the aircraft came, thirty of them, flying in a long string, like migrant geese, low over the beach. There came also barges loaded with drums of fuel, with tents and stores and bombs. Shank's cart was busier than ever and he began to believe that it was this and not the sand that he was hired to haul. He thought it was nice of Billie Mitchell to pay him off every night after supper, when the grown-ups waited until the end of the week to get their money. Shank Austin preserves some of the pieces of money he received at the hands of one of the most controversial figures of his generation.

On Wednesday, September 5, 1923, as military officials and news reporters watched in another plane, the large De Havilland DH-4 and small Martin MB-2 bombers noisily took off. They had been equipped with newly developed bombsights and supercharged engines. Mitchell watched from yet another plane. Many villagers had left the day before, afraid the bombs might accidentally be dropped early. Now, others also went into hiding.

The planes flew toward Cape Hatteras to the north and spotted the USS *New Jersey* and the USS *Virginia*, battleships that were required to be destroyed under the treaty ending World War I. The first round of bombs missed their targets. But within 30 minutes, eight planes flying at an altitude of 3,000 feet and deploying 13 bombs weighing 1,100 pounds each sank the *Virginia*. Then three Martin bombers dropped three bombs to sink the *New Jersey*. The two ships were at the bottom of the sea.

Mitchell and his men were given a celebration by the locals in Hatteras that afternoon, including a barbecue on the beach.

Back at Langley Field in Virginia, Mitchell wrote that night, "Spent practically the entire day in the air watching the bombardment of seacraft. After each flight I returned to the airdrome and issued instructions. The tests were completed successfully." Though the exhibition had pointed out problems to Mitchell, it achieved its goal. As David Stick writes in *The Outer Banks of North Carolina*, "The success of this experiment established Mitchell's claim that aerial bombing was essential in modern warfare."

It did indeed, though the acknowledgment was hardly immediate. The results were unequivocal, but army officials remained unenthusiastic. In the meantime, Mitchell's criticism of his superiors, often before Congress, became increasingly strident. Finally, in late 1925, he was court-martialed for insubordination and "conduct prejudicial of good order and military discipline" and suspended for five years. Instead, he resigned in January 1926.

Mitchell, it turned out, would be proven right again.

Following a trip to Japan in early 1924, Mitchell had submitted a report foretelling a Japanese attack on United States forces in the Pacific. A Japanese air and sea attack would be launched at Pearl Harbor, followed quickly by an air attack in the Philippines, he said. "Attack will be launched as follows: Bombardment, attack to be made on

Ford Island (Hawaii) at 7:30 A.M. . . . Attack to be made on Clark Field at 10:40 A.M."

Such an attack did not come for 17 years, five years after his death. But Mitchell was prescient. On December 7, 1941, the Japanese attacked Pearl Harbor at 7:55 A.M. and Clark Field in the Philippines at 12:35 P.M. Mitchell had erred by only 25 minutes for Hawaii and less than two hours for the Philippines.

Mitchell's vision finally received official recognition a decade after his death. In 1946, Congress posthumously awarded him a Special Congressional Medal of Honor. The only such medal ever bestowed, it set the record straight. Inscribed on the front was, "Brigadier General Billy Mitchell." On the back was, "Award of the Congress August 8, 1946 for outstanding pioneer service and foresight in field of American military aviation." The United States Air Force, a separate branch of the military, was established the following year.

His court-martial, meanwhile, became the basis of a 1955 Otto Preminger movie, *The Court-Martial of Billy Mitchell*, starring Gary Cooper in the hero's role.

On Hatteras Island, Mitchell was not forgotten. In 1953, a North Carolina historical marker was cast for placement near the northern entrance to Buxton. The marker reads, "Billy Mitchell, 1879–1936. Brigadier general of the Army Air Service, demonstrated air power by bombing battleships off coast, Sept. 5, 1923. Landing field was here."

Moreover, in 2003, the Graveyard of the Atlantic Museum in Hatteras Village opened its largest exhibit, on Mitchell. It includes photos from the 1923 Hatteras bombing tests and the radio shack he used to direct them.

The display at tiny, wind-swept Billy Mitchell Airport near Frisco features pictures of a Martin bomber and the two ships sunk by Mitchell's flyers, the USS *Virginia* and the USS *New Jersey*.

It also includes a 1933 quotation from Mitchell predicting the superiority of aircraft in the skies and beyond: "My children in their lifetime will see aeronautics become the greatest and principal means of national defense and rapid transportation all over the world and possibly beyond our world into interstellar space."

Turns out he got that right as well.

Chapter Eleven

A NATIONAL SEASHORE

I t is hard to imagine Hatteras Island without Cape Hatteras National Seashore. Without the park's dunes, sea oats, and wild birds—and especially its building ban— the island would be peppered, if not covered, with duplexes and strip malls.

It once was hard to imagine Hatteras *with* the national seashore. The nation's first seashore park was not established until 1953, nor dedicated until five years later, but it was on the radar screen for more than a generation, so difficult and contentious was the prospect.

Elizabeth City Independent publisher W. O. Saunders was an early advocate of making the entire coast of North Carolina a state park. "A Coastal Park for North Carolina" appeared in his paper July 21, 1933, during the depth of the Depression. The article was written by the plan's creator, Frank Stick—artist and father of future Outer Banks historian David Stick—who combined the pursuits of real-estate development and conservationism. The plan would set aside large natural areas, as well as the entire coastline, though an island-long highway also was anticipated.

The notion was audacious. "It was an idea bold in conception for its time and found but a few people with sufficient vision or interest to grasp its possibilities and its worth

Much of Hatteras is part of Cape Hatteras National Seashore and thus is undeveloped for miles upon miles. The only views are of Pamlico Sound and the Atlantic Ocean, perhaps with a glimpse of one of the villages in the distance. Founded in 1953, the nation's first seashore park includes 30,000 acres on three islands—mostly on Hatteras.

Photograph by Vicki McAllister

to the people," newspaperman John Morgan wrote later.

It found enough, however, and had a strong ally in Congressman Lindsay C. Warren. By the 1930s, Warren enlisted support. Depression-era funding first began to go to out-of-work men, directed by Stick, for restoring Hatteras Island's eroding beaches and putting up fences to catch and hold the drifting sands. The National Park Service joined in the restoration. Stick also began persuading a few large landowners to donate island acreage to the state, which would hold it for the federal park.

Meanwhile, fence lines were installed on the beach, creating three lines of dunes from the Virginia border down

It's called a seashore park, but as this aerial photo shows, much of it is wooded, particularly here near Cape Hatteras, at the widest point of the island. The lighthouse is in the lower left, while the cape itself is near the top of the photograph. Beyond the cape, the treacherous Diamond Shoals extend into the Atlantic Ocean.

Photograph by Laura Sturtz, National Park Service

the length of the Outer Banks to the end of Hatteras. Tom Carlson, writing in *Hatteras Blues*, describes what opponents would come to see as the problem:

> The new dunes were planted with cordgrass, sea oats, American beach grass, and wire grass, all of which propagated through rhizomes—creeping stems that grew underground and anchored themselves in loose, shifting soil. The dunes continued to grow as they were built, many to a height of fifteen feet, and the project seemed a rousing success. The only trouble was that as the dunes rose, the shoreline receded. The gently sloped beaches, once 150 yards wide, had narrowed to half that. The reason was simple physics. Storm waves and storm surge, no longer able to overwash dunes or to shoot between them and thereby dissipate their energy and deposit their sand inland, found themselves crashing into a highway of sand. The wave energy was then hurled backward and

downward onto the beaches in front of the artificial dune wall. Such massive energy thus directed had the effect of gouging the beach, deepening its profile and narrowing it as the sea crowded into the excavated area.

The beach is still there. Beach restoration eventually would be scrapped during the 1970s but it came to a temporary halt during World War II—though not because the wisdom of the program was reconsidered. Rather, German submarines were off the coast, firing deadly torpedoes at American ships. That pushed dune stabilization down the list of the nation's wartime priorities.

The interlude could have derailed the park project altogether. Oil companies began buying up mineral rights during the war. Islanders started to think the oil industry might offer better employment opportunities than a seashore park. In 1945, the state legislature stopped land acquisition. Everyone agreed, David Stick wrote later, that the park now seemed dead. "Dad's dream, apparently, had been only that. Just a dream."

But exploratory drilling turned up little. Standard Oil Company dug an 8,500-foot-deep well near the lighthouse in 1946, bringing in rigs, a seismograph unit, and explosives. Two big diesel engines worked day and night, in the end finding only a trace of gas. They also discovered ancient bugs fossilized in shale.

By 1949, the Sticks and supporters had allies in the Interior Department and the area's new congressman. The seashore park might be alive again. Frank Stick had helped persuade the family of Henry Phipps and others to donate land. Four nonresident landowners—J. S. Phipps, J. H. Phipps, Winston Guest, and Bradley Martin—donated 999 acres around the Cape Hatteras Lighthouse. The land was essential.

Most may not know it, but the island's beaches, even within the villages, are part of the national seashore park. Thus, fishing piers lease their property from the park. This beach access is in Salvo in front of the Old Richmond *shipwreck, seen in the distance.*

Photograph by the author

Prospects still were dim, however. Bickering continued. Public meetings brought out opposition. The project's size was scaled back slightly, the existing seven villages were excluded, and the government agreed to build Highway 12.

Even so, the idea was a tough sell. The federal law authorizing the seashore guaranteed residents "the right to earn a livelihood by fishing" in the park but subjected them to regulations necessary to protect it for recreation. Moreover, National Park Service director Conrad L. Wirth, in a letter to the *Coastland Times* in 1952, promised locals that the service and its staff "stand ready to cooperate with you at all times in the development of your communities, if you want us to. I hope we can work together as partners, and that we can look forward to a long and pleasant association." Wirth added that the National Park Service would protect dunes, beaches, and beach access.

Finally, in June 1952, two foundations associated with Andrew Mellon offered to put up $618,000 to buy land if the state of North Carolina would match the money. Four days later, it did. The park soon opened. It included 30,000 acres on Bodie, Hatteras, and Ocracoke islands—a 72-mile-long stretch of oceanfront property.

The impact was immediate and profound. The new park took up nearly two-thirds of Hatteras Island, making it a singular place, perhaps for all time. Gary Dunbar, in *Geographical History of the Carolina Banks*, wrote in 1956 that it would break the pattern of development by preserving what tourists valued most:

> Ironically, in a seaside area, the property most highly prized is that which was of least value prior to the advent of tourists—the beach itself. This sandy waste, the portion of the Banks most vulnerable to storm damage, has the two features, sand and sea water, which constitute the prime attraction of the area to tourists. . . . The acquisition by the

National Park Service of all the Banks [oceanfront] from Whalebone Junction south to Ocracoke Inlet prevents the repetition there of the pattern established in the Nags Head–Kitty Hawk area.

Many property owners, however, remained against the park. "The seashore park met with opposition from the beginning, mostly from those who feared loss of profits from real estate," Morgan writes. "Those opponents, sometimes by misrepresentation of the actual possibilities of the park, aroused anti sentiment among others, but most came to see that the Seashore Park actually hurt nobody but was a great boon to the entire Outer Banks."

Most did, perhaps, but certainly not all. The park abandoned dune restoration efforts in 1973, allowing nature to take its course. Buxton resident Bill Dillon was one of many who complained, saying that the National Park Service was "bent on letting the ocean come over and do whatever it feels like doing. . . . We are truly locked in a battle for survival with the Park Service."

In 1974, anger arose over the park service's proposal to ban commercial fishing along Cape Hatteras on weekends in January, February, and March. Some islanders thought that a violation of the park's agreement to allow fishermen a right to earn a living.

Four years later, problems with erosion led the park service to propose beach driving restrictions that proved unpopular, especially among villagers who thought erosion could be dealt with better by building jetties, a new inlet, or artificial reefs.

Perhaps the biggest dispute came three decades later, this time over driving restrictions related to protected species like the piping plover and the leatherback sea turtle, which nest on the island. The park service was developing an off-road-vehicle management plan, with input from community and interest groups, when environmental factions stepped in and filed a lawsuit in 2007. The next year, a federal judge approved a temporary solution—supported by fishermen, off-roaders, and other groups—that required the park service to step up protection efforts until it could develop a complete plan in 2011. The park service had to block off larger protected areas. It had to restrict nighttime driving for half the year.

Those restrictions set off a firestorm on the island. Opponents began staging rallies, gathering petitions, posting signs, writing letters to newspapers, and engaging in whatever other forms of protest had an effect.

The struggle continues. Many see the national seashore as the great savior of the island. Others view the National Park Service as the great intruder. The park service admitted as much in a 2008 notice, saying, "Many business owners fear a negative economic impact from the loss of access to prime surf fishing spots. Residents are concerned about the loss of their traditional use of the beach. Protected species advocates fear loss of species without the intervention of the court."

The park service hopes the various groups can help develop a plan that "brings to closure decades of conflict and uncertainty [over off-road vehicles] and protected species management at the seashore."

Irene Nolan, a longtime newspaperwoman who now edits an online news site, has been on Hatteras for nearly two decades. She says the beach closure issue is a powerful one for the islanders, who feel ganged up on. "How it's going to play out is going to have an enormous effect on the island and the people who live here," she says.

Nolan sees both sides, but particularly that of islanders who feel overregulated. "I think [environmental] special

Near the cape itself, often called Cape Point, fishermen, water enthusiasts, and other beachgoers drive onto the beach to spend the day. Historically, beach access was unlimited on Hatteras Island. Vehicles of all types have driven the sands for nearly a century. Now, however, concerns over endangered species, erosion, increasing population, and other matters have led to lawsuits, restrictions, and confrontations.

Photograph by Vicki McAllister

interest groups have taken over the leadership of the National Seashore. . . . I've been an environmentalist. In the 1970s, I was a long-haired hippie [protesting] about phosphates. . . . But I have never been more embarrassed by the environmental movement."

A workable compromise seems the likely result of the beach driving issue, as with most conflicts between islanders and the park service. No one wants open warfare on the beach, after all. But mistrust and hard feelings seem likely to remain.

For good or bad—most likely, good *and* bad—the seashore park has created a unique atmosphere on Hatteras Island. To those not directly affected by the controversies, it remains a wonder in a world where developers seem to hold the upper hand. Elsewhere on North Carolina's barrier islands, once-natural settings are being taken over by resorts, souvenir shops, and duplexes built to the legal limits. It is sometimes difficult to distinguish a beach town from a suburban strip—other than for the knowledge that somewhere out there, beyond the duplexes, is an ocean.

Hatteras, by contrast, offers a setting other islands could provide now only with a time machine. The island mostly remains populated by just grains of sand, strands of sea grass, various forms of wildlife, and what water overwashes it all during storms.

This is a beach still. This is an island still. This is nature still.

Ignatius "I. D." Midgett thinks those who opposed the park service's taking beach land have been proven wrong. "Everybody was dead set against the park service when they tried to come down here. I could be numbered among [them. . . . But] now the only thing I'm sorry of is that they didn't take more." Midgett says the only big problems are with developers. "They'd like to have all the beach so they could build some more mini-hotels out there."

Even some of those who acknowledge that the seashore has preserved a way of life harbor mixed feelings. "The park service saved us from ourselves," one islander says. However, he continues, "the park service is not great—their public relations is awful. It's like they show up with a club with a nail driven through it to try to soothe people's feelings. But hell, independent of that, where would we be? We could be Nags Head."

Chapter Twelve

HIGHWAY 12

The Outer Banks are sometimes referred to as "a ribbon of sand," and if that description is apt, calling the single highway that runs the length of Hatteras Island "a string of asphalt" is equally so.

Apt, but hardly sufficient.

There may be no more magical roadway than Highway 12, or at least none better suited to delivering the soul from an ordinary life. South of the crowded beaches at Kitty Hawk, Kill Devil Hills, and Nags Head, the multilane U.S. 158 departs the Outer Banks, leaving tiny North Carolina Highway 12 to go it alone the rest of the way south.

It is early morning, and the sun rebounds off the Atlantic Ocean, glimpses of which can be caught by the driver—or all of which can be breathed in by pulling over and climbing to one of the dune crossovers. If a storm has passed recently—and when is this not the case on Hatteras?—puddles are likely to be here and there on this magical means of conveyance. The sun glistens off them. Approaching motorists, if there are any, slow to lessen the impact.

The first thing one sees on the island is the old Oregon Inlet Life-Saving Station off to the left, for which renovation lies ahead. On the right up ahead is Pea Island National Wildlife Refuge. The island seems not to have changed in a century.

For most of its inhabited life, Hatteras Island has had no Highway 12. Indeed, no paved road at all. No asphalt, stone, or gravel. Only ever-shifting sand. Newcomers can scarcely imagine such a time, not even after a storm that leaves the roadway invisible under a blanket of sand.

Before Highway 12 was "the Old 101"—that is, 101 different sand tracks that always moved. You picked the one that looked firmest packed and hoped you got through. Sometimes, it was called "the Old 108." Same road.

The best route was down by the water, the firmly packed, wet part of the beach called "the wash." But that was available only at low tide. The farther up the beach the tide progressed, the farther up the beach you had to drive—and the worse off you were. No one wanted to drive up near the dunes. They called that "the bank," which was the softest part of the beach, the part with all the dry, shifting sand. In fact, big trucks usually avoided the beach altogether, choosing instead to drive an "inside road" (or "the Inside") nearer the sound, where the villages were. Cars took that route, too, if the wash wasn't available.

John Morgan, a newspaperman and public official who grew up during the Depression, spent summers with his grandparents at Hatteras Village. He remembers in his 2001 autobiography, *A Pleasant Gale on My Lee*, that it was a full day's drive from his home to Whalebone Junction beyond Nags Head. Morgan continues,

> At this point you could take a right and go over to Manteo and spend the night, or keep heading south to Oregon Inlet where Toby Tillett operated a four-car ferry. A narrow sand road could be traversed after debarking

Tillett's craft. If you happened to be going down on low tide, you could take to the low-water mark on the ocean side and make much better time. Otherwise, one had to negotiate the sandy road where more than likely one got stuck three or four times before arriving at one's destination, and it was "get out and push!" Prior to starting on the trip down the beach one would always slacken the tires by letting out air. All autos of this era carried a hand pump and a patch kit for repairing flats.

A local legend on Hatteras was "the Pepsi-Cola man" of the 1940s and early 1950s. Soda was popular on the island as an alternative to the low-quality drinking water of the day. The Pepsi-Cola man trucked his wares from Elizabeth City on the mainland, traveling across the sound on the ferry and then down the spine of Hatteras on those sand "roads." He brought along two-by-eights or two-by-12s that he had found on the beach. "We'd be going along," his son, a commercial fishermen turned charter boat operator, remembered years later, "and the sand would get real soft like it does in the summertime. . . . He would have to pull those boards out from underneath that truck and start 'boarding' his way. He'd take one board and go a little ways, and another board."

Getting stuck was always a possibility unless you had four-wheel drive. Gibb Gray, an Avon man born in 1927, received an army surplus truck from his father in his youth. Most vehicles would struggle, but Gray could keep moving on the sand roads. Making good time, however, was another issue. "To make it to Buxton, you could only make about eight or ten miles an hour," Gray said in a park service interview. "To give you an example, they had a theater in Hatteras [Village], Austin's Theatre. . . . The movie took in about 7:30 P.M. If you wanted to see a movie in Hatteras, you would have to leave here about four o'clock in the

Hatteras Island was wild and remote—parts of the interior almost impassable—until a highway was built in sections from 1948 to 1952. Before then, drivers of vehicles like this truck, circa 1935, had no choice but to make a road of the beach. It could be slow going.

N.C. Office of Archives and History, Outer Banks History Center

afternoon, and it was around 12 o'clock before you got back that night, just to go see a movie. . . . You could go from here to New York in about that many hours."

In 1946, North Carolina writer, editor, tourism director, and geographer *extraordinaire* Bill Sharpe compiled some of his favorite pieces in *Tar on My Heels*. In "Hatteras Highway," Sharpe anticipated the coming of a paved road down the narrow island, based on a one-mile experiment then being conducted from Whalebone Junction near Nags Head to Oregon Inlet.

Sharpe correctly predicted—mostly, anyway—that a Hatteras highway ultimately would lead to all sorts of "progress," from license plates, speeding, and crime to lawyers, traffic lights, and magazine salesmen. He also described those final days of a pre-asphalt way of life:

> Outsiders who go to the Banks might love isolation, but the Bankers themselves don't love it, and get no pecuniary profit from it. Most of the residents not working for the Coast Guard are fishermen, and they have to freight the fish to market by boat, and they say that a fast and dependable road will substantially increase the convenience and profit of their calling. Thus the Bankers themselves, by dint of their necessity and their appeals, seem likely to do away with the placidity which is one of the chief charms of the Banks. . . .
>
> If the experiment at the Whalebone withstands high-tides and drifting sand, or can even be reasonably maintained against their depredations, then it is planned to extend the sand-and-asphalt surface down the sandbank to serve such ancient and solid communities as Rodanthe, Waves, Avon, Frisco, Salvo, Buxton and Hatteras. At present traffic down the 50-mile beach proceeds at low tide along the beach ("the wash"), or in the sandy ruts locally known as "the Inside." No matter which route you elect, you always wish you had chosen the other one, though experienced sand drivers get along fairly well.

This 1940s Hatteras driver heads down "the Old 101." Before Highway 12, old-timers will tell you, there was "the Old 101"—that is, 101 different sand tracks. Sometimes, it was called "the Old 108."

Photograph by John Hemmer, from Bill Sharpe's 1946 book, *Tar on My Heels*

> The Inside is a highway by custom and usage only. It
> has no legal right of way, no maintenance, and the route
> partly varies according to the sand drifts, the sound tide, or
> the whims of the first ferryload of drivers across Oregon
> Inlet who manufacture the day's first tire marks.

Locals had waited for the road since they began paying road taxes in the 1920s. But Hatteras was always put off. Governor Melville Broughton made a trip to the island during World War II, the year after an island delegation had visited Raleigh to push for the road. Appropriately enough, Broughton's motorcade got caught in the sand. The governor himself had to get out and push. Still, no road was immediately forthcoming.

Work finally got under way in 1947. There were easier places to build a road. That December, a barge carrying trucks, a Caterpillar tractor, and other equipment sank in nine feet of water off the road's edge. A diver and huge cranes were needed to retrieve the equipment.

Even laying asphalt was difficult. The asphalt base necessarily included sand—a combination not altogether efficient when building a highway on sand. So, rather than laying the asphalt mixture hot, workers made it a liquid instead with the addition of naphtha, a flammable mixture more often used as a solvent. When the naphtha evaporated, the asphalt remained in place.

Since materials were most easily delivered via Hatteras Inlet, the road was built in sections from the south: the 17.3 miles from Hatteras Village to Avon in 1948, then 17.8 miles from Avon to Rodanthe in 1950, and finally the 12.4 miles from Rodanthe to the tip of the island at Oregon Inlet in 1952.

Islander Les Hooper recalled helping haul the tar on Tillett's ferry for that final leg of paving. The tar was pumped into trucks. Then the work crew, he said, "just put the tar down on the sand and ground it up with a machine. In hot weather, if you stopped your car on it, you would just sink right down and get stuck."

Even after the asphalt was laid, Highway 12 was hardly impervious to the elements.

Stocky Midgett was one of three brothers who took over their father's Manteo-Hatteras Bus Line after he died in 1938. The brothers operated it until 1973. The bus line ran the length of the island, leaving Hatteras Inlet at 8:15 in the morning, making a stop in each village, and usually arriving after about four and a half hours to take Toby Tillett's ferry across Oregon Inlet and head on up to Manteo. Then the bus made the return trip. In the days before the road, the bus would drive along the Hatteras Island surf if the tide was out, or along the bank or the beach on the best of the "101" roads if the tide was in, avoiding deepwater cuts and driving around shipwrecks. Even after the road was built, drivers encountered problems. Stocky Midgett one day almost lost a bus. He remembered the story years later:

> I was driving to Manteo one day after we had the highway. The ocean tide was coming across the road south of the old Coast Guard station, and the bus motor drowned out. I got out on the front bumper to dry the distributor, trying not to get my feet wet. Meanwhile, the front wheels just fell through the road. I hurried to get the people out and put them on a hill. I had to practically swim [to the Coast Guard station] but I got there. We took the "duck" [amphibious vehicle] back to where the bus used to be. We couldn't find the bus. The bus was completely covered.

Those who thought that paving the Old 101 would stabilize it have proven only partially correct. The asphalt highway hasn't stayed still either.

The Manteo-Hatteras Bus Line, shown here in 1946 in Hatteras Village, was a lifeline, especially before the highway was built. The bus, run by three brothers in the Midgett family, left Hatteras Inlet at 8:15 in the morning, driving the beach and stopping in each village. It reached the ferry crossing at Oregon Inlet about midday, continued to Manteo, then turned around and made the trip back to Hatteras. Ironically, the company almost lost a bus after the highway was built, as it sank through the road during high tide one day and disappeared.

Aycock Brown Collection, Outer Banks History Center

Hatteras remained a lonely and rugged island after Highway 12 was built, as this 1955 photograph of the village of Frisco shows. Still, travelers now had a brand-new highway and could travel the length of the island with relative ease most days.

Aycock Brown Collection, Outer Banks History Center

Ralph Crumpton, a fisherman who visited the island beginning in 1962 and now lives in Avon, says the road is still at the mercy of the elements. "Highway 12 has been moved about five times," he says, standing on the Avon Pier and taking a rough accounting in his head. Each time, it has been pushed a little farther from the sea. No spot, Crumpton suggests, should be considered permanent—not on this island. "Mother Nature's going to do what it's going to do," he says.

Everyone on Hatteras understands the truth of that claim. Nonetheless, the magical road is usually open and in great demand. Sometimes too great. On summer holiday weekends, cars jockey for position, many impatiently passing one another to arrive five seconds earlier at their destinations. And not just motor vehicles use the only north-south road on much of Hatteras. Walkers, joggers, and bicyclists join the parade, too, dangerously clinging to an almost nonexistent shoulder as cars speed by. The time to add safe pedestrian and bicycle paths in the villages seems near.

As predicted, Highway 12 has been a huge catalyst for change, first leading to the consolidation of small village schools into the Cape Hatteras School in Buxton in 1955. When the Herbert C. Bonner Bridge over Oregon Inlet was completed in 1963, it made the ferry obsolete and effectively opened the island to more tourism and development.

The paved road and the bridge changed Hatteras culture—speeding it up, in essence. One Waves woman notes an irony resulting from the timesaving highway and bridge. "I spend all my time in the car," she says. "If I want anything, I'm usually up the beach or in Manteo to get it, and sometimes I go three or four times a week, which takes a lot of time. You didn't do that when you had to catch a ferry."

They noticed the change at the Burrus Store down in Hatteras Village. Before the road and the bridge, customers

Part and parcel of the building of Highway 12 was the opening of the Oregon Inlet bridge—the Herbert C. Bonner Bridge—in 1963. The bridge, shown here in a postcard not long after it opened, made the ferry obsolete and opened the island to more tourism and development.

Author's collection

After a typically heavy Hatteras storm, Highway 12 just above Rodanthe is clogged with sand. Heavy-equipment operators work feverishly to remove it. When the work is complete, the road is passable again, even if the canyon of sand is a little intimidating.

Photographs by Vicki McAllister

came to the grocery store by boat from Ocracoke Island to the south and from as far up the island as Avon. Within a decade, the road "brought a lot more people and made it easier for us to come and go and changed our way of life right much," W. Z. Burrus said in a 1974 magazine interview. "We have less time on our hands than we did then. It seemed like we had more time to ourselves."

A Hatteras Village resident recalls how tourists looking for the lighthouse would wind up down in her village, comically exasperating her grandfather:

> When they first paved the road, we'd sit on his front porch, and people would get lost. They'd be looking for the Cape Hatteras Lighthouse. My grandfather, I'd see him wrinkle up his face and say, "You drove all the way down and you didn't see the Cape Hatteras Lighthouse up there in Buxton? Do you know that lighthouse marks some of the most dangerous shoals in the world?"
>
> I'd say, "Oh, Papa, please be nice to these people."
>
> And he'd say, "They coulda run aground and killed theirself."
>
> And I'd say, "Papa, that's a car! That's a Studebaker!"

Confused tourists and accelerated lifestyles aside, much of the island remains the same as it was decades ago.

A 1952 magazine piece by Sharpe, by this time writing as Highway 12 neared completion, harked back to the 1920s, 1930s, and 1940s. Yet he seemed to describe an environment similar to that of today:

> Those first 20 miles of driving from the ferry had a lot to do with determining whether you were suited for the Outer Banks or not. No matter where you went, the dull roar of the surf always was in your ears. Except for Pea Island Coast Guard station (until recently manned by the only all-negro life guard crew in America) there

was not a habitation in that first 20 miles. There are no "rural" people on the Banks. Simple and inconvenient as life is on the island, it is no place for hermits, and people live in tight little villages—seven of them—all located on the sound (west) side. It is not possible on the Banks to get very far away from the ocean, but the villagers are as far from it as geography permits.

For the most part, they spent their lives on that side, so as you drove down the Banks, you had an ocean and a beach all to yourself. It is a beautiful beach, highly exposed and disturbing under the threat of a hurricane, because it offers no hope of shelter, but benign on a sunny day and under a moderate wind. . . .

This is largely a barren island and the elements are as often stern and forbidding as they are pleasant. With the exception of Trent Woods, Hatteras is as exposed as the deck of a ship uneasily anchored in an uneasy sea.

No one with the slightest historical perspective would confuse the Hatteras Island of today with that of three-quarters of a century ago. Highway 12 has been the primary carrier of change. Yet the skinny two- and three-lane piece of asphalt has also opened a world of wonderment to visitors who would never have seen it otherwise.

It is perhaps best traveled in the off-season when few are about, when one might not see a vehicle for miles. The Hatteras highway offers a different experience each time to those looking for it, whether early in the morning or late at night. Waves crashing to the left. The sun setting over the sound to the right. Storms appearing over the dune line. Sea gulls gliding over the dunes. Shorebirds posing for pictures atop them.

Those who see Highway 12 only as transportation, only as a means to getting someplace quickly, do so at their loss—and pay the price. It is a roadway that can move at a maddeningly slow pace during the summer, especially within the villages.

Yet somehow, it always seems to take one off the island too quickly.

Traffic on Highway 12 can move slowly on a busy summer holiday. Most times, it is a highway of solitude.

Photograph by Vicki McAllister

Chapter Thirteen

BARD OF THE BANKS

D avid Stick looks out over Kitty Hawk Bay, then ventures onto the dock that extends from his backyard. It is a remarkable scene, a small gazebo at the end of the dock, with water, birds, and Colington Island beyond. "I built the railing and the gazebo 10 years ago," he tells a visitor. It seems the perfect touch.

This is the type of place you would imagine David Stick would live.

Stick came to live on the Outer Banks in 1929, when his parents moved from New Jersey to Roanoke Island, and he has hardly left since. He was not yet 10 years old. His father, Frank Stick, was a renowned artist who somewhat paradoxically became a real-estate developer and investor. Furthering the paradox, Frank was an environmentalist who played a major role in the development of Cape Hatteras National Seashore, thereby removing 30,000 acres of

Bodie, Hatteras, and Ocracoke islands, including 70 miles of shoreline, from potential development.

The Sticks knew the beauty of the Outer Banks, in other words.

It was a hunting friend who invited Frank from New Jersey. "He went down there and fell in love with the place," David says of his father. Frank also knew the land would be worth something one day. He and associates eventually picked up options on 14 miles of ocean-to-sound property, most of it on Hatteras Island, his son says.

As he tells the story, Stick pauses to deal with a couple of honking geese that have wandered onto the property. "What are you yelling about?" he asks them. He knows precisely what they want. He and his guests spread cracked corn for the geese.

Stick actually had seen the Outer Banks before his family moved to them, spending the summer of 1928 across the bay from where he is now. Indeed, something that happened later that year represented his first brush with history. The Wright brothers had flown four miles from where he lived. On December 17, 1928, a celebration was held for the 25th anniversary of the first powered flights. Orville Wright, the lone living brother, was the principal attraction.

David got to attend the celebration. "I caught a ride in a truck, and a nice lady was holding me in," Stick says, pausing slightly before delivering the kicker. "Amelia Earhart."

The next year, after the family had moved to Roanoke Island, David traveled farther down the Outer Banks and saw Hatteras Island. Frank drove his son from their home at Skyco down the length of Hatteras to Hatteras Village. No bridge to the island existed, nor a Highway 12. David remembered that first drive fondly and vividly 77 years later, writing in his straight-ahead style for *Our State* magazine:

Dad was an experienced sand driver, and [soon after] we reached the Nags Head end of the wooden Roanoke Sound Bridge, he deflated the tires, flattening them out so they had a tendency to roll over the sand instead of digging in.

The sea was relatively calm and the tide falling, which meant there was an area of hard-packed sand above the wash. Getting there seemed to be the problem, but Dad revved up the car engine, kept his wheels in the tracks others had made, and managed to drive over the dune without getting stuck. Once we reached the beach, he seemed to drive as fast as the car would go on this no-speed-limit oceanfront highway.

They rode across Oregon Inlet on a flat towed by a commercial fishing boat. The craft rose and fell on giant swells, an exhilarating ride. Frank and his son drove the beach halfway down the island, passing shipwrecks and Coast Guard stations. At Cape Point, near the lighthouse, they turned inland to Buxton Woods, driving sand trails beneath overhanging branches and passing occasional residences and even a few stores. Out of the woods, they hit the bare stretch of beach between Frisco and Hatteras Village. Stick continued,

Dad chose to take the inside route instead of driving the wash, for the tide was coming in. The sand was soft and dry, so he tried to keep in an earlier track, but when we met a car coming from the other direction, he had to pull over, with his left wheels in the right wheel track, even as the other driver made the same maneuver. Both cars got stuck, and the occupants of each helped push the other, as Hatteras Islanders had from the time the first automobiles appeared on their island.

The trip to Hatteras Village was the beginning of Stick's love affair with the island, one that would pay dividends for generations of readers and others. "In the ensuing years,

Stick, shown here in 1988, took his first trip to Hatteras in 1929 as a boy, riding the length of the road-less island with his father. They deflated the tires for traction, then drove at breakneck speed along the beach. "In the ensuing years," Stick wrote in 2006 for Our State *magazine, "I made that trip innumerable times, always with the same feeling of excitement and awe."*

Photograph by Drew C. Wilson, Outer Banks History Center

David Stick, at home in a striking location on Kitty Hawk Bay, is best known as the chronicler of the Outer Banks. He was also one of the early developers of the Banks, though a conservationist as well. "I retired in '76," he says now. "By then, I thought that every change that could possibly happen had taken place." He laughs at the preposterousness.

Photograph by Vicki McAllister

I made that trip innumerable times, always with the same feeling of excitement and awe," he wrote. His classic book *The Outer Banks of North Carolina, 1584–1958*, which came out nearly three decades after the trip, was dedicated "to my father Frank Stick whose love for the Outer Banks is contagious."

By 13, young David was selling a brand-new magazine, *The State*, going door to door. It proved a fortuitous introduction, as Stick has written on and off for the magazine, now *Our State*, for nearly three-quarters of a century.

At 15, he was writing "Nags Head News and Notes" for the *Elizabeth City Independent*. By 16, he was a bureau manager for the *Elizabeth City Daily Advance*. He was also a stringer for the Associated Press and one day fired off a bulletin saying two people had been killed in a plane crash at Nags Head. He then went to work on the story for the *Daily Advance*, which would print it on the front page. That must have been heady stuff for the youngster, for he forgot all about the Associated Press—that is, until his forgetfulness was made an object lesson in the AP's national newsletter for stringers. The article was accusingly entitled, "How Not to Cover a Plane Crash." Nonetheless, Stick's writing career seems not to have suffered.

He briefly attended the University of North Carolina. "I flunked out of college my first year," he says straightforwardly. The following fall, he left to hitchhike the country, taking in Florida, California, Washington and New England. Later, he nonetheless would receive a Distinguished Alumnus Award from the university, which called him "living proof that education does not stop at the schoolhouse door."

The hitchhiking trip did not go to waste either, becoming the basis of his first magazine piece, "Hitchhiking 9,000 Miles," which ran in *The State* on January 21, 1939. His writing career was under way.

During World War II, Stick spent four years in the marines as a combat correspondent. He went on to become associate editor for *American Legion* magazine.

Afterward, he began work on what would become one of his best-known books, *Graveyard of the Atlantic: Shipwrecks of the North Carolina Coast*. Finding resource material was difficult. He traveled to New York, Washington, D.C., Raleigh, Chapel Hill, and elsewhere, tracking down out-of-print books, old manuscripts, maps, and papers. "I learned how antiquarian booksellers can find things for you, when I was in New York," he says. He also learned something else. "I didn't have the money to spend the night in a motel," he says. "At that point, I realized I needed to build up a library." More often than not, he would buy the materials, beginning a massive collection. A decade later, he became an antiquarian book dealer himself, selling books so he could buy others.

At the same time he was researching, Stick was involved with real estate and conservation, like his father. He became the Outer Banks' first licensed real-estate broker in 1947, helped develop the Southern Shores planned community, and worked on North Carolina's trendsetting Coastal Area Management Act. There ended up being a practical aspect to the combination of historical research and real-estate development. "I was developing what is now the town of Southern Shores, which Dad started," Stick explains. "I was building houses, and so I built my own 6,600-square-foot house filled with books."

Four decades later, he donated that personal library, by then the largest collection of North Caroliniana outside the University of North Carolina, to the state. It became the basis for the Outer Banks History Center at Manteo. The collection included more than 25,000 books and pamphlets, along with 150 cubic feet of correspondence, business records, and research notes. Another way to measure his contribution is by linear feet on bookshelves: 10 feet on shipwrecks, 37 feet on Sir Walter Raleigh's Roanoke colonies, 14 feet on the American Revolution, 35 feet on natural history, 48 feet of biographies, 23 feet on education, eight feet of colonial records, and so forth.

Stick's way of measuring is more practical. "There are people over there all the time who are using my library, and I'm very proud of it," he says.

Like almost everyone, Stick laments excess development on the Outer Banks, which has overtaken northern locations more than it has Hatteras. Even he is surprised. "I retired in '76," he says. "By then, I thought that every change that could possibly happen had taken place." He laughs at the preposterousness.

As a youngster, Stick intended to write the Great American Novel and still has the unpublished manuscript in his attic. He also wrote a short local history, *Fabulous Dare: The Story of Dare County Past and Present*, borrowing $14,000 to publish it in 1949. His book career was thus launched. *Graveyard of the Atlantic*, which began as part of an Outer Banks history until Stick decided to write it separately, followed. It went on to sell more than 100,000 copies. Stick's dozen books have sold a combined total of well over a quarter-million.

There is a rich irony in David Stick's being the foremost historian of the Outer Banks. "I never passed a history course," he says. "Didn't like history. But I was exposed to history here."

That history included the early English settlement on Roanoke Island, of course. Moreover, the Wright brothers made their flights on property later owned by Frank Stick and a partner. When they sold it, the deed contained a provision that a piece would be reserved for a memorial. One was dedicated in 1932, and Orville attended that ceremony as well. By the time David Stick moved to the beach in the late 1930s, he saw firsthand what it meant. "Almost every plane that came by," he says, "would circle the memorial in tribute to it." Pride is in his voice as he speaks.

Stick is not the only one to write of the Outer Banks, of course. Hatteras and the rest of the barrier islands have been the setting for any number of novels, historics, and travel guides. Stick is one of at least three well-known writers whose nonfiction works on the Outer Banks have gained generations of acclaim. The others are both deceased: Ben Dixon MacNeill, whose artfully written *The Hatterasman* preceded Stick's *The Outer Banks* by a year, and Judge Charles Harry Whedbee, who wrote five popular volumes of Outer Banks legends and folklore.

Stick has no problems with Whedbee's books. But he loathes MacNeill's work, which he says "purports to be history but isn't. . . . It's not nonfiction, it's fiction—a lot of stories, mostly told by Coast Guard men."

His disdain for MacNeill, whom he calls "a crazy old hermit," began when *Graveyard of the Atlantic* was being reviewed in newspapers. Stick's meticulously researched book said just over 600 ships had wrecked in the "Graveyard." MacNeill wrote a column in a Raleigh newspaper claiming 2,400 ships had gone down within sight of the Cape Hatteras Lighthouse. Stick says that error came from MacNeill's extrapolating a total from just one month of shipwrecks—the month when German submarines were doing their worst work during World War I. Stick confronted MacNeill: "He tells me, 'Dave, I don't mind using facts as long as they don't get in the way of the story.' " In 1969, *National Geographic* published a piece about the treacherous shores and their shipwrecks and produced a famous map, "Ghost

Fleet of the Outer Banks," that is still framed and sold in many shops. The magazine called upon Stick to help document the shipwrecks but, he says, used the erroneous 2,400 number.

Stick goes to one of his home's myriad bookshelves, pulls down a copy of *The Hatterasman*, and reads from Mac-Neill's foreword: " 'I am not a historian and this is not a history.' " He puts the book back. "That's Ben Dixon," he says. "By God, that's Ben Dixon." He pauses to acknowledge that MacNeill writes beautifully, better than he. "But that book's caused me a lot of grief. People will read the stories and then come to me, 'Why didn't you tell that

Stick, a man of both books and the outdoors, signs a copy of one of his classic works, The Outer Banks of North Carolina, 1584–1958. *On the table are vintage photographs and another of his favorite books, a collection of his father's art,* Frank Stick: Splendid Painter of the Out-of-Doors.

Photograph by Vicki McAllister

story?' " Stick says he immediately responds, "Because it *never happened*!"

His annoyance brings to the fore two of Stick's most pronounced traits: his insistence on accuracy and his unabashed cantankerousness. He admits to having a temper.

Another trait is his involvement with the community. In 2007, as he was approaching his 90s, Stick was given the first Living Legends of the Outer Banks Award. The audience's ovation was not only for his role in developing and promoting the region but also—perhaps primarily—for his lifetime of caring. Stick has been on more boards, commissions, and foundations than he can count, and he has often run up against his fellow developers.

In his short acceptance speech, Stick talked about work done from earlier days—like getting telephone and police service—to more recent efforts. "It was strictly a team effort, with the same people serving over and over again . . . ," he said. "I guess the reason I'm up here is that I think all the rest of them have already passed on, and that's the best I can figure out."

The line drew a laugh. But as David Stick sat down, everyone knew the historian, the stickler for fact, had gotten that one wrong.

Chapter Fourteen

THE TRI-VILLAGE
RODANTHE, WAVES,
SALVO

D rive down Highway 12 past Pea Island and you come to three villages—first Rodanthe, then Waves, then Salvo. The uninformed might not distinguish one from the other—they merge seamlessly— and the lack of village signs at the borders kills any chance of doing so. Locals blame surfers and beachgoers, who keep stealing the Waves sign.

But historical differences among the villages are strong. A 19th-century traveler would have had no such difficulty. The three were distinct settlements, separated from each other by about two miles, the small creeks between them crossed by bridges.

The names—now, those were a different matter.

The three villages were considered part of the Chicamacomico area. Initially, Rodanthe was called North Chicamacomico. Waves, the middle town, was South

Chicamacomico. Those two northern villages maintained a close relationship, even sharing a post office until 1939. The southernmost village of the three, Salvo, was known as Clarks or Clarksville.

But the names were always fluid. What you called the villages depended on who you were or where you lived, or who your family was, or who you knew.

North Chicamacomico also was known at various times as Big Kinnakeet, Chichinock-Cominock, Chicky, Midgett Town, and Northern Woods. The official change from North Chicamacomico came in 1874. The United States Postal Service set up an office and refused postmaster Sparrow Pugh's request to keep the long Indian name. Actually, he requested Chickamacomico, with a *k*. No one is sure of the origin of the name Rodanthe, but that's what the new post office became. Thus, the village was known then as North Rodanthe, while South Chicamacomico became South Rodanthe. Mail for all three villages was dropped off daily by boat. The mailboat continued to what is now Avon and then to Hatteras Village.

Meanwhile, Clarks, which got its own post office in 1901, became Salvo. The name apparently came from a Union ship commander—or so the story goes, and it's a good one—who spotted the community while heading north and asked the crew for its name. The charts showed none. "Give it a salvo anyway," the commander ordered. His men fired the cannons, and one of the sailors noted "Salvo" on the chart. Others then began using it on their maps as a name. The post office followed suit, mercifully rejecting the name Phlox, suggested by new postmaster Kenneth R. Pugh. The reasons for suggesting Phlox have been lost to history, but how good could they have been?

Meanwhile, when South Rodanthe got a post office in 1939, Anna E. Midgett became postmaster, running the

Rodanthe—pronounced Ro-DAN-thee—was called North Chicamacomico and a variety of other names until 1874. The village was isolated, its life revolving around fishing, the lifesaving station, church, and several general stores. The village is shown here in 1952, the year Highway 12 was built from Rodanthe north to Oregon Inlet, finally completing the island-long road.

Aycock Brown Collection,
Outer Banks History Center

service from her house. She chose the name Waves, and the postal service had no problem with that. So South Rodanthe became Waves—actually, "Waves P.O." to most—and North Rodanthe settled into plain Rodanthe.

The post office was an important part of the community. One villager recalled rushing to the new Waves post office early every day to visit residents for the mail call. "The best thing was you knew each piece of mail everybody got," she said. "The postmaster would call out the names of every piece of mail so you knew who got a letter and who got a package. The packages were usually from Sears Roebuck or Montgomery Ward." Today, the only active post office in the Tri-Village is in Waves.

All the changes are only part of the confusion over names.

Rodanthe Pier owner T. J. Cary says that visitors invariably mispronounce the name of the northern village. It should be Ro-DAN-thee, but the correct pronunciation is no better than the third most used. "They call it everything," Cary says. "Ro-DANTH. Even Ro-DANT. But it's Ro-DAN-thee. The name is Indian, not English. It means cattle." Adding to the confusion, some old-timers used to pronounce it Road-Anthony.

So, for the record, it's Ro-DAN-thee, Waves, and Salvo. And if you can tell where each begins and ends, you're probably a local.

Enough about names. Historically, life in the three villages was simple. Simple but hard. Most everyone was involved in commercial fishing, though usually as a part-time job. The men set their nets, went on to something else, and then came back to check them. They launched small skiffs in Pamlico Sound or set their nets for bluefish, summer flounder, trout, and mackerel. Across the island, in the ocean, they sank nets offshore or worked from small beach

Waves shared a close relationship with Rodanthe but not with other island villages before Highway 12 was built. This aerial photograph from 1956 shows just how narrow Hatteras is and how small and isolated Waves still was. "If you was out in the sound in a boat," a villager said, "and looked back at the shoreline, you would see three clumps. And you knew Waves was the middle one." Now, Rodanthe, Waves, and Salvo—the Tri-Village—all run together. If you can tell where one ends and the next begins, you're probably a local.

Aycock Brown Collection,
Outer Banks History Center

Waves was named by postmaster Anna E. Midgett once the village was awarded a post office in 1939. Midgett ran the post office from her home until she retired. This photograph from 1965 shows the second of the five locations, in the right-hand side of a building also housing C. A. Midgett's general store. For the record, Coca-Cola did not sponsor the post office.

Aycock Brown Collection,
Outer Banks History Center

dories for spot in September and then for speckled trout, striped bass, and puppy drum in late fall and early winter. Most fish buyers were in Rodanthe. A couple of small fish houses were in Salvo, but none were in Waves.

If someone had a real job in what is now the Tri-Village and it wasn't in commercial fishing, it was most likely at the Chicamacomico Life-Saving Station once it opened in 1874, or at the Coast Guard station after its conversion in 1915. Members of many families—including, famously, the Midgetts of Rodanthe and Waves—worked for the Coast Guard for generations.

Children went to village schools, at least until those in Waves and Salvo closed in the 1930s. At that point, they began attending the Rodanthe School. (That school, in turn, closed in 1953, following the paving of the island-long road, after which all the island's children went to school in Buxton.) They would come home to play on the beach, run with the wild horses and cattle, and watch rescue drills at the lifesaving station.

"We had something here as children that probably very few places in the world have," one islander says. "We had total and absolute freedom because the island was more or less sealed off from the world." It had no roads, no electricity, no amenities—but parents had peace of mind.

Churchgoers went to the Episcopal, the Methodist, or later the Pentecostal church on Sunday, then often shared dinner with neighbors.

A popular spot was the general store—or general stores, plural, as several small ones owned by Rowan Midgett, Sudie Payne, Asa Gray, and the Hooper family existed a century ago.

T. Stockton Midgett started a store in 1936 initially to serve Civilian Conservation Corps workers building dunes on the island. There were no hours per se. The store opened more or less when someone needed to buy something. Residents bought on credit and paid at the end of the month.

The Hooper family had several stores in Salvo through the first half of the 20th century. Aaron Hooper's small store in the 1920s and 1930s was a gathering place on Sunday afternoons. It, too, was often closed, being essentially a storehouse that responded to residents' requests.

Asa Gray's store was more often open. Men gathered in the afternoons at A. H. Gray General Merchandise, located in Waves where Real Kiteboarding is now. Rudy Gray, born in the 1940s, remembers post–World War II times. "My grandfather's store," Gray says, "sometimes there would be 10 or 12, 14 men there in the afternoon sitting around talking, some of them playing dominos, checkers, and stuff like that." The Grays had one of the few radios on the island, and that, too, was an attraction. "The radio was over to my great-grandparents' house behind the store," Gray says, "and that's where they would gather to listen to those boxing matches at night."

Islanders a century ago traveled by foot, horseback, horse cart, or boat. Cars appeared at Chicamacomico in the 1920s. Private ferries soon followed for those wanting to drive north off the island and on to Manteo.

Stockton Midgett's teenage sons took over his bus line to Manteo in 1938 and went on to operate it for 35 years. They were a godsend. A Hatteras villager remembered, "You had guys that were 15 or so, and they were running a bus service, and no one in the community thought that it was odd or strange or somehow wrong or they needed to be regulated. It was, 'Thank God someone's running a bus!' They were a couple of enterprising kids who could do the job."

Many of the same families populate the villages as have for centuries: the Midgetts, O'Neals, Meekinses, and Grays in Rodanthe and Waves, the Paines, Hoopers, and Grays in Salvo.

But many others have moved in, too. Summer cottages and other rental homes now fill most of the Tri-Village. The most expensive are new, large rental homes near the ocean. Those are the prime lots for vacationers and developers. "Back in those days, people didn't build on the ocean," Waves villager I. D. Midgett says simply. "They just knew that it was foolish. Everybody built on [the sound] side. They knew eventually it was going to wash away over there. . . . The bulk of their livelihood was on this sound. There wasn't all that much fishing in the ocean. Most of their fishing was done in the sound."

Roads, technology, and the influx of people have changed the Tri-Village—but not as much as one might suppose. One of the most noteworthy events on the island, and almost surely its least understood, is Old Christmas in Rodanthe. Old Christmas, celebrated January 5, or more recently on the Saturday closest to January 5, has its beginnings in 1742, when England adopted the Gregorian calendar and shortened the year by 11 days.

Jan DeBlieu, in her 1987 book, *Hatteras Journal*, notes that the celebration is planned for local residents. Although visitors are welcome, "they seldom grasp the significance of the event. Moreover, many tourists are reluctant to attend, for Old Christmas has the reputation of being a drunken brawl." Though it once was customary for Hatteras men to settle their grudges with a fistfight after dinner on Old Christmas, DeBlieu writes that the celebration itself has had only a few sparring matches, excepting those times when out-of-towners have come looking for fights.

Initially, the event had religious overtones, but many became lost in the merriment—and the strangeness. Old Christmas often began with music from homemade fifes and drums, played by villagers leading a procession of Sunday-school members. One member of the Payne family beat a pre–Revolutionary War drum. Villagers joined in until the procession reached a large feast. The children took part in a pageant. A large dance was, and still is, held.

Old Christmas traditionally began the night before, on January 4. Villagers often have worn costumes, men dressing as women and women as men. In the era before racial sensibilities, some wore blackface as minstrel performers. The costumed went door to door the night before Old Christmas, begging for food for the feast and sometimes stealing chickens.

About midnight after Old Christmas ended, villagers would gather on the beach to watch the "weird action of the cattle," as Virginia Midgett related in a 1979 *Sea Chest* magazine article: "[The cattle] would fall on their knees at midnight and make low murmuring noises as if they were praying. The people believed this was the proper time to celebrate because the animals played an important part in the nativity. After the cattle dispersed and returned to the grassland, the folk would begin their journey home, stopping at several different houses for hot coffee and cold sweet tater pie."

Old Christmas continues today. The celebration usually includes an "oyster shoot," the target-shooting winner earning a half-bushel or so of oysters. Sometimes, the shooting exhibitions have had higher stakes. Virginia Midgett reported that, years ago, one captain at the lifesaving station used a .22 rifle to shoot six apples, one by one, off the head of a surfman. Fortunately, he was a good shot.

And Old Buck, a now-mythical wild bull, always makes an appearance. Old Buck was said to have been the only survivor of a shipwreck off Rodanthe. Brought ashore to impregnate every cow in Buxton Woods, he was shot by a

Rodanthe's Old Christmas, one of the most singular festivals imaginable, is celebrated annually in January. Here, festival-goers take part in the oyster roast on January 8, 1972.

Aycock Brown Collection, Outer Banks History Center

farmer one day. Now, he reappears at the dance as a cow's head and skin nailed on a two-by-four or two-by-six, two men hidden below. Old Buck is always eager to kick and buck his way around the dance floor.

Old Christmas may seem oddly out of place, but it is a genuinely authentic festival, harking back to the island's early civilization. A 2005 report on the island prepared for the National Park Service summarized it thusly:

> Old Christmas has the feel of attending someone else's family reunion, not only because most of the attendees are kin, but also because some of the customs are foreign if not inscrutable to the visitor. . . .
>
> Participants and organizers walk a tight rope between the modern and the traditional [suggesting] that Old Christmas is, among other things, a ritual of cultural pride and resistance on the Outer Banks. It is through long-standing cultural events, such as Old Christmas, that participants express their pride in who they are, where are they from, and the history and traditions that, despite hardships, have been passed down. In refusing to relinquish their unusual rite or make it innocuous enough to suit the visitor's palate, Rodanthe villagers staunchly resist the forces of homogenization that are transforming coastal areas with an unprecedented degree of wealth and tourism.

The Tri-Village has become a combination of past and present. Almost everywhere are small signs of a bygone era.

Just off the beach at Salvo, directly across from the dune crossover that leads to the Salvo Inn Motel, the sun glistens off a curious rusted piece of metal rising from the surf. The motel owner explains that it is from the *Old Richmond*, a 19th-century steamboat that went down off the brutal coast of Hatteras. She knows because the story has been handed

Through the years, the shoreline of Hatteras has been littered by shipwrecks, including that of the Old Richmond, a 19th-century steam vessel or side-wheeler. The propeller shaft—easily visible off Salvo, particularly at low tide—is a local landmark.

Photograph by Vicki McAllister

down in her family, generation by generation. No official record exists.

Some locals go further in their perhaps fanciful description, claiming the *Old Richmond* burned offshore and littered the beach with bodies during the Civil War. Calmer accounts say it was a steamship operating in 1878 and that the visible portion, which appears to be the boat's anchor, is actually its propeller shaft.

Regardless, for years, the ancient boat has sat in the Salvo surf, withstanding the pounding waves and punishing storms of Hatteras. It has become a guidepost, a civic landmark. Few who walk by with a camera can resist taking a photograph. An illustration even graced the cover of the Salvo Volunteer Fire Department's cookbook.

Other landmarks have disappeared. The new intermingles with the old.

Rodanthe used to be heavily wooded. A wetland called Aunt Phoebe's Marsh stood between Rodanthe and Waves. The area is now the site of a campground and of a water slide and go-cart track that are part of a large amusement park. Rodanthe may have changed the most of the three northern villages. Restaurants and shops line Highway 12. Surfers and kite boarders are likely to be parked nearby.

Down at the south end of Waves, a fenced-off cow pasture along the sound once doubled as an airstrip. Among those who used it was a Manteo doctor. "The Piper Cub landed in that," Lance Midgett recalled, "and the pilot stayed to keep the cows from licking it to death while the doctor made calls." The pasture is now occupied by an upscale housing development called Wind Over Waves.

Perhaps the most photographed scene in the Tri-Village, other than the Chicamacomico Life-Saving Station, is the teeny-tiny Salvo post office, which opened in 1901. It still sits alongside Highway 12 near the south end of the village,

Salvo's tiny post office was only eight by 12 feet, sat on rails, and was moved by villagers whenever a new postmaster took over. It shared the award for the nation's "Smallest Post Office" in 1988, four years before an arsonist set it afire and the postal service decommissioned it. Now restored, it sits alongside Highway 12 as a reminder of a different time, sometimes confusing would-be postal customers.

Photograph by Vicki McAllister

though it has not been in use for years.

The structure earned a measure of fame when it tied for first place in a national "Smallest Post Office Challenge" sponsored by the California state government in 1988. The eight-by-12-foot white building was so petite that it sat on rails and was moved by villagers whenever a new postmaster took over. Inside, gilded boxes surrounded the service window, itself so small customers could see only the postal worker's midriff. "I'd talk to them and they'd say, 'Yes, ma'am, yes, ma'am,' " former postmaster Edward Hooper recalled. "And when I'd come around to the door, some of them had the funniest look on their face. They didn't know [I was a man]." Hooper, postmaster for nearly half a century, also recounted another story:

> A woman come up to that little hole and she looks and says, "Is this a bathroom?" "No, ma'am, lady. This is the post office." She did the same thing again. She says, "Is this really a bathroom?" I say, "No, ma'am, lady, this is the post office." Well, the third time she rub me the wrong way. She was just making fun. I said, "Lady, you see all these bushes out round the back of this post office? If you need to go to the bathroom, you help yourself. That's where I go!" She didn't have to use the bathroom anymore.

No move was ever made to construct a bigger post office, even though Salvo's had no air conditioning—or, obviously, bathroom. So when the quaint little building was set afire by an arsonist in 1992, the postal service decided to decommission it, even though the building was quickly restored. It was moved to Hooper's front yard—and placed on the National Register of Historic Places a year later.

Passersby often stop for photos of the famous tiny white post office with red and blue trim. An American flag usually flutters on the pole nearby. "People still come by wanting to mail a letter," Hooper said. "Some of them stick letters under the door."

On Hatteras, the old ways die hard.

Chapter Fifteen

AROUND THE CAPE
AVON, BUXTON, FRISCO

B uxton Village Books is exactly the type of business one would expect, and hope, to find on Hatteras Island—warm and inviting from the outside, with a parking lot a shade too small, and even cozier inside, where visitors wind among the cramped aisles, looking for a coastal book or the latest bestseller to take to the beach.

It may look like the type of tiny business that could be blown away by the next big wind or the next economic downturn, but it survives because it is someone's passion. Everything on Hatteras is someone's passion.

The Outer Banks have almost always been a part of Gee Gee Rosell, the shop's owner, and she almost always a part of them. Her family vacationed at Nags Head when she was growing up. "Even in the '70s, Nags Head was too crowded," she says more matter-of-factly than critically.

When she came out of college in 1974, Rosell went to work for Eastern National, helping set up souvenir shops in the national parks on the Outer Banks. When she left that job, she knew only that she wanted to stay in this place somehow. She had been a forestry major at West Virginia University, limiting her options on Hatteras, one would think. But she had taken a lot of English classes, too. "The only thing I knew was literature," she says. A bookstore seemed as good an idea as any.

She found a little 300-square-foot building at an intersection alongside Highway 12 and carved a shop out of it. "The center two rooms were a detached kitchen," Rosell says. "As I needed more room over the years, I added rooms." She means that quite literally. She didn't pay someone to add rooms—at least not for the most part. She added them herself. "I learned how to frame rooms and wire," she says. A carpenter and electrician of necessity, she now has a 1,200-square-foot store.

<hr/>

It is a good place to be. Buxton is at the center of Hatteras Island.

Avon, Buxton, and Frisco are the island's three interior villages, all in proximity to the cape—the "elbow" of the right-angled island, as it is sometimes called—and its famed lighthouse.

Coming down the island from the north, after leaving the Tri-Village and driving through the national seashore, one first encounters Avon. This was one of the island's earliest settlements, extending from Buxton Woods to Salvo. It was known as Kinnakeet, an Algonkian word meaning "that which is mixed," a reference to the English and Native American populations. The Kinnakeet post office opened in 1873, a tiny outhouse-sized building representing a halfway

This undated photo, possibly from the 1960s, shows the quiet life of a street in Avon.

Aycock Brown Collection, Outer Banks History Center

point in the route to Hatteras Village.

Ten years later, the village's name was changed to Avon. But villagers clung to Kinnakeet for generations. They still do—or some do, at least. The old name even appears on the Avon village sign as "Historically Kinnakeet." The village itself has been surrounded by residential and commercial development yet remains nearly unspoiled, tucked off the highway near Pamlico Sound, opposite the Avon Pier.

Thanks to the area's abundant live oak and cedar trees, boat building flourished in Kinnakeet from colonial times until after the Civil War. The village was the economic center of the island, at least until the opening of Hatteras Inlet in 1846 passed that distinction to Hatteras Village. The boat-building industry faded as trees were overharvested. A massive "sand wave" then invaded the area, the large dune moving hundreds of feet per year from the ocean to the sound. By 1890, it covered the remaining forests and even unearthed graves.

Before that time, and for a good while afterward, most men of the village fished or otherwise relied on the waters. Their boats crossed the sound to the mainland carrying oysters, salted spot, and mullet. They returned with corn or wheat to be ground at the village mill—at least until windmills disappeared early in the 20th century—or sorghum molasses and salt pork.

The seas were bountiful, but this being Hatteras, life was not easy. One old-timer remembered living as a child at Little Kinnakeet, the lifesaving station north of Avon. This was during a bitter winter around 1914. The sound froze, she said, and many were hard-pressed to survive. Men from other villages, unable to launch their boats or ride horses on frozen ground, arrived looking for food and supplies. The residents gave what they could. "The people up to Rodanthe had eat their food up," she explained. "Two men walked down from Rodanthe and took up on their back what food they could."

It was an insular world. Many Avon men were employed by the Coast Guard. They, almost alone among the locals, did see a bit of the world. One married a 17-year-old girl he met in New York and brought her to Avon in 1932. What she found, the woman said seven decades later, was a shock:

> No roads anywheres—sand car ruts, and the cattle and horses were roving free. After we bought the old church and moved up here, the outhouse was back there in the marsh and there was no trees; it was all the saltwater grass. I went to the outhouse, and when I turned to come back there was this old brindle bull between me and the house, and I was stuck out there for about two hours. He was a gentle old thing, but I was from New York. And I didn't know nothing about gentle bulls.

For entertainment in Avon, the residents had, well, swimming and not much else. "No traffic on the beach. We'd just pull off our clothes and go naked," another villager recalled. "See a car coming from a long distance, we'd go in the ocean and let it pass. And we swam in the sound. Lots of crabs, things that make swimming the sound inconvenient and painful at times."

The only thing resembling an amusement park ride came when sea tides overwashed the island from the ocean to Pamlico Sound. "You could swim at great speed with the current from the ocean coming down through these creeks," the villager said.

A boat captain named Loran O'Neal transported iron ore to Maine during the 1920s, then switched in 1927 to running a freight boat up the sound from Avon to Elizabeth City and back. The profitable business lasted until his primary boat, the *Missouri*, was destroyed in the 1944 hurricane.

O'Neal also had a Coca-Cola franchise. He delivered Coke, NuGrape soda, RC Cola, and Double Cola throughout the island, along with the freight. "They called Cokes 'dopes' back in those days; Coca-Cola had cocaine in it until 1937," O'Neal's son, L. P., said years later. "We used to have a big garage like a warehouse, and it was always stacked with drinks and things." Loran O'Neal's wife, Ida Mae, collected money from island stores, often with children in tow. According to her son, "she didn't take no bull off nobody." She never had trouble collecting from Chicamacomico stores, but Buxton and Frisco—now, those were another story. One store owner ran out the back door when she approached. She tracked him down and got her money.

In addition to boat building, Avon had small industries for processing yaupon tea and seaweed. Seaweed was harvested, processed in a local factory, then shipped to New York to make mattresses.

Big news came in 1952, when boatbuilder Willie Austin constructed the 20-room Avon Hotel, the second such facility on the island, following the 1920s-era Atlantic View Hotel in Hatteras Village. State senators and other prominent guests sometimes spent the night, but most of the Avon Hotel's guests were fishermen or salesmen from the mainland.

Shopping was limited. Families walked to Avon stores for flour, cornmeal, sugar, coffee, lard, beans, peas, canned tomatoes, and canned beef. No fresh eggs, meat, or bread was available. Villagers were on their own for those, says one woman who was brought up at the Little Kinnakeet Life-Saving Station. "I was telling somebody a few days ago, down at Food Lion, this old man. I said, 'What do you think these old people would do, walk in Food Lion and see all this food?' My God, they couldn't believe it!"

Like most of Hatteras Island's villages, Kinnakeet and Trent received new names when they got post offices or shortly afterward. Kinnakeet received its post office in 1873 and became Avon a decade later. Its post office is shown here around the 1950s.

Aycock Brown Collection, Outer Banks History Center

Trent became Frisco when it got a post office in 1898, the new postmaster purportedly naming it for his favorite city, San Francisco. The Frisco office is shown in 1965, when it was part of the Pirate's Chest store building.

Aycock Brown Collection,
Outer Banks History Center

Avon today has not only the Food Lion grocery store but a large, bright yellow Wings T-shirt and souvenir store, a movie complex, and a True Value hardware store. None of them is as important to the community as were the old-time stores and their owners, however.

Gibb Gray's general store, which operated from the mid-1920s to the mid-1960s, was one of the larger ones in Avon. Gray's iron safe held not only his valuables but the savings of his neighbors, according to an oft-told story. When the massive hurricane hit in 1944 . . . well, let Ben Dixon Mac-Neill tell the story. This is an excerpt from his 1958 book, *The Hatterasman*:

Even my neighbor Gibbie Gray can and does now laugh at what happened to him that day. He is a merchant, and in his store there was, and is, a very heavy iron safe. It contains mostly the savings of his neighbors, a bond or two in a packet, some money in another. Anything that they want to keep in a place that is reasonably safe from fire or like hazard. On that day, when the waters came, and the 140-mile wind—Gibbie Gray thought there must have been in the neighborhood of sixty thousand dollars in money or securities, the lifelong savings of his neighbors. There were no banks.

With houses floating around like worried ships Gibbie Gray got to worrying about the contents of that safe. If the store floated away, it would carry the safe, and then where would he and his neighbors be? He dumped it all into a heavy sack and lashed it to his back and started home. Before he got there he was overtaken by surging water that now, astonishingly, was coming from the Sound. The wind had shifted and the sea receded. But the Sound came up even higher. The water's surge lifted Gibbie Gray and his burden upward. He caught the lower limb of a massive liveoak that has been standing in that village for a good half millennium. He took firm hold and climbed. He attained a place of comparative safety halfway up, and he settled down there and rode out the storm.

Afterward, he hauled his store back to where it belonged and restored the contents of the safe to its keeping, and the savings came in very handy when his neighbors began to retrieve their houses from wherever they had happened to lodge.

Next down the island is Buxton. The village, known to tourists mostly as the home of the Cape Hatteras Lighthouse, is also the site of Dare County offices, local schools, a number of motels and restaurants, a campground, and, of course, prime fishing at the cape.

Early maps identified Buxton as Cape Hatteras Indian Town, for the Native Americans who once lived near or camped at Cape Hatteras. East Carolina University archaeologist David Phelps and others reported finding European trade items at a site in Buxton. A 1788 deed transferred the "Indian Town" site from "Mary Elks, Inden" to "Nathan Midyett."

By the time the community's post office—the island's second, after Hatteras in 1858—opened in 1873, the village was called "The Cape." The name Buxton was chosen nine years later for local judge Ralph P. Buxton.

Though Diamond Shoals, offshore from Buxton, are treacherous, the village is more protected from storms than others, thanks to its being 10 feet above sea level, tucked into the wooded area of Cape Hatteras. Many people have moved from Avon to Buxton after facing storms and flooding.

Buxton's border merges with that of Frisco, once known as Trent or Trent Woods. Indeed, the village is still heavily wooded, which is a curse and a blessing both. With the moist woods come mosquitoes and ticks but also a sense of privacy. Though it has a fishing pier, a Native American museum, restaurants, a campground, and even art galleries and a nine-hole golf course, Frisco seems almost undiscovered. Indeed, a real-estate sign down the road in Hatteras Village proclaims, "Best Buy: Frisco."

Like Buxton and unlike Avon, Frisco is considered relatively safe from storms and flooding. Its series of sand dunes, known as Stowe's Hills, protected Union encampments during the Civil War. The largest, Creeds Hill, was the site of a lifesaving station.

The name change to Frisco came in 1898 with—surprise!—the establishment of a local post office. Postal authorities rejected Trent, apparently not wanting confusion with a town of the same name on the mainland. The first postmaster, a man named Wallace, was an avid traveler who had—surprise again!—shipwrecked off Hatteras and married a local woman. He suggested the name San Francisco, for one of his favorite cities. The postal authorities accepted the shorter, colloquial version instead.

Frisco once was a satellite community of Buxton, thriving until the opening of Hatteras Inlet shifted economic activity down to Hatteras Village. Frisco's population of 205 in 1910 diminished further to 126 by 1940. With tourism, it was up to 845 by the year 2000.

A local woman, Connie Farrow, described growing up in the village in the 1920s for the 1976 issue of *Sea Chest* magazine:

> You could listen to the ocean's roar and tell pretty well what direction the wind would be the next day. You could tell by the sunset whether it would be rainy or clear. You could walk down the road in the early morning and hear people grinding their coffee beans. You could smell such a sweet aroma from the fresh boiling coffee. Another sound we miss is the chopping of wood. Everyone burned wood in those days and even the smoke from a

wood fire smelled good. We also miss the honking of the geese and the cranking of the brant [a species of goose].

"The main thing our fathers used to do was gather at Mr. A. J. Fulcher's store at night," Farrow continued. "It was interesting to listen to the stories they could tell. Around nine o'clock, they would leave and go home. Mr. Fulcher's store was located about the center of Frisco, so some of the men had quite a long way to walk. From far away, you could hear some of them strike up and sing."

Frisco was known primarily for two products in its early years: firewood and yaupon tea. The latter, made from a member of the holly family, was used as a patriotic substitute for British tea during the Revolutionary War. Production peaked during the Civil War, when harbors were blockaded.

Today, businesses in the three villages in the middle of the island are geared as much to tourists as locals. Gone are boat making, yaupon tea processing, firewood sales, and seaweed harvesting.

Relying on tourists, however, can make for tough going three-quarters of the year.

Gee Gee Rosell's Buxton Village Books has done steady business for a quarter century of summers by selling fiction, local history, coastal books, children's books, and the like. The midnight release of the final Harry Potter novel in 2008 drew 400 people, most waiting outside in the middle of the night, winding around the corner of the building.

Still, running an island bookstore is not exactly a get-rich-quick scheme. Other such shops have come and gone, not quite working out the dynamics of making enough money during the summer to cover the rest of the year.

"I don't think anybody would open a bookstore if they looked at the financials," Rosell says. "All Hatteras Island

Buxton Village Books is exactly the type of business you would hope to find on Hatteras: small, quaint, and run as someone's passion.

Photograph by Vicki McAllister

has maybe 20 percent of the number of people a bookstore would need to survive." The census says nearly 5,000 people live year-round on the island. It's really closer to 3,000, she says.

Rosell survives because she wants to. There is something very "Hatteras" about that. It reflects the way islanders have persevered and sometimes thrived in an often inhospitable environment. She keeps the shop open 73 hours a week during the summer, hiring part-time help. "I have a very loyal local following," she says. Many choose to buy books from her, even if they could do so more cheaply online or at off-island shops.

The rewards are more than financial, then. Rosell has the advantage of doing what she wants, where she wants. Among the perks, she counts "meeting people who read and talking to them about the next book they want to read." Many of her ideas on what books to stock come from customers.

She admits it might be nice to add a coffee shop, though, as large bookstores off the island have, and as some vacationers have requested.

But it would have to be coffee only, then. She would have no room for books.

Chapter Sixteen

THE FISHING PIERS OF HATTERAS

I t is a warm late-September morning, the temperature reaching for the low 80s, the wind mild, the clouds on sabbatical. The weather is too good, almost, for this time of year, and though the big crowds of fishermen will not arrive on Hatteras until next month, enough have come out to give the piers a sense of excitement. There is no better place to be than a fishing pier.

Ralph Crumpton sits in a bag chair about midway out the Avon Pier, poles in the water, a smile on his face. He likes this place. The Avon Pier is like a gentle roller coaster, full of soft S-curves, angling from side to side and up and down, an inviting, if irregular, construction. The fishing is good.

Crumpton has been here, on and off, for nearly 50 years, ever since the pier opened in 1962. He was just 18 at the time, a high-school senior but already an avid fisherman. He had begun bass fishing in the '50s on Currituck Island. Then he and his brother moved south to Oregon Inlet, then farther south still. In the years since, he has fished up and down the coast. He fell in love with Avon. Once he retired as a meat cutter for the Harris Teeter grocery chain, Crumpton made it official and moved here.

This is a fisherman's paradise, of course. Hatteras Island has long been known for world-class fishing and sportfishing. Crumpton credits the closeness of the Gulf Stream. The Gulf Stream, flowing from the south, and the Labrador Current, flowing from the north, meet at Cape Hatteras. They bring migrating fish in both fall and spring, so the variety is continual.

"This is more laid back, a place to get away from things," Crumpton says. He has been talking about Burlington and Myrtle Beach, and it is clear that Avon serves as a counterpoint. "I come to get away from the hustle and bustle."

Three piers stand on Hatteras, at Rodanthe, Avon, and Frisco. All are far from the hustle and bustle. Rodanthe's pier house is built into the bank, like many others in North Carolina; Avon's and Frisco's, with less land, are elevated well above the beach. The piers were all constructed by the early 1960s, in essence leasing their beach space from the national seashore. They have all gone through several sets of owners.

The piers of Hatteras have something else in common. They have all been whacked by storms. Each has been repeatedly repaired and rebuilt. Each is shorter than its original length. Nothing, especially fishing piers, trifles with the storms of Hatteras.

Like piers up and down the coast, those on Hatteras are endangered. "These three piers are some of my favorites to fish," says Al Baird, president of the North Carolina Fishing Pier Society. "We spend three weeks on Hatteras a year,

The Hatteras Island Fishing Pier, shown here most likely in the late 1940s, drew visitors as part of the Hatteras Island Resort, which included a motel, a restaurant, and cottages. Most of the resort was destroyed by a 2003 hurricane, but the pier remains. More often known now as the Rodanthe Pier, it is the farthest point east in the southern United States.

Aycock Brown Collection, Outer Banks History Center

Ralph Crumpton sits in a bag chair along the Avon Pier, enjoying a laugh. The beach is eroding, Crumpton will tell you, and the pier is sinking. No matter. He wouldn't be anywhere else.

Photograph by Vicki McAllister

and I fish each of them when I am there. Having said that, I think these piers are in the worst shape of any piers in the state. I am afraid of a self-fulfilling prophecy. . . . But if a storm would take any of these piers, I do not think they would be rebuilt."

Only time will supply the answer to that hypothetical. What is certain is that storms will play a part in the piers' futures. They certainly have in the past.

The Rodanthe Pier, originally and sometimes still known as the Hatteras Island Fishing Pier, was built in the mid- to late 1940s. The 1,100-foot structure lost much of its length to the Halloween storm of 1991, according to the North Carolina Fishing Pier Society. It was still 850 feet long early this century, but the Thanksgiving Day storm of 2006 reduced it to 639 feet. Of course, pier measurements are inexact science. The pier's owner says the Thanksgiving

Day storm took out 52 feet, and that the pier is still 796 feet long.

The pier at Rodanthe may or may not be the island's longest. It is, however, almost certainly the best known. It was a focal point of the regionally famed Hatteras Island Resort until Hurricane Isabel wiped out the resort in September 2003, even detaching the pier house from the pier—though, oddly, leaving the pier intact.

The island's northernmost pier also gained a modicum of fame for its cameo role in the 2008 movie *Nights in Rodanthe*. And even at its reduced length, the Rodanthe Pier has a noteworthy claim to fame: the end of the pier is the farthest point east in the southern half of the United States.

The next pier down the island is Avon's, which opened in 1962 at 927 feet in length. Woody Jones, working the counter at the Avon Pier this day, says, "It's 600 feet now. It was 700-some. In the 1970s or 1980s, a hurricane knocked off 100 feet." The missing portion was not replaced, though the end of the pier was rebuilt as a T. The North Carolina Fishing Pier Society, which measured the three piers in 2006, says the Avon Pier is 756 feet long.

The pier farthest south—and the only one beyond the bend at Cape Hatteras—is the Frisco Pier. Built as the Cape Hatteras Fishing Pier in 1960, Frisco's was the shortest of the three on the island, measuring 600 feet. Now, it is just 560 feet long, according to the society. A pier house worker contends it's even shorter—that it was 525 feet long until Hurricane Isabel took out 82 feet, since replaced, in 2003.

Whatever its length, Frisco's tiny pier looms large in other regards. "Talking to the locals on the piers, Avon and Rodanthe do not bring in the number of large fish, excluding big red drum, because . . . anglers cannot reach past the outer [sand] bar," says Baird. "Frisco seems to not be affected as bad and tends to catch its fair share of kings [king mackerel]. But they do catch large drum and large bluefish as well."

The three piers offer mostly the same species, though small seasonal differences do exist, mostly because the Frisco Pier is south of Cape Hatteras and the other two are north. Though fishing is virtually year-round on Hatteras, the fall months are the best, bringing trout, spot, puppy drum, sea mullet, red drum, and a variety of others. The spring months are not far behind. Few who fish go home without a haul—and usually a photograph or two documenting it. All three pier houses have walls of fading Polaroids of the biggest catches over the years.

Some of the catches have been oddities—a Maine lobster at Rodanthe, for instance, and a scalloped hammerhead shark at Avon in 1993. But many are mind-boggling simply because of their size. World records are not uncommon on Hatteras. Jack Scott caught an 82-pound channel bass at the Avon Pier on November 9, 1970. James Hussey caught a 32¾-pound bluefish on the island in 1972. (John Hersey's book *Blues* claims the world-record bluefish was caught on the Hatteras Island Fishing Pier, but Baird says he doesn't think Hussey's was caught from a pier.) Elvin Hooper caught a 92½-pound red drum at the Rodanthe Pier on November 7, 1973. And exactly 10 years later, on November 7, 1983, David Deuel broke Hooper's record with a 94-pound, two-ounce drum caught on the beach just north of the Avon Pier.

World records all.

The Hatteras Island Fishing Pier was built in the 1940s by Dickie Ferrell, who maintained it until the mid-1990s, says current owner T. J. Cary. The exact construction date is unclear. Regardless, the pier is both historic and an important part of the island's character.

It is evening on a moonless night. Cary is standing in the pier house of what is usually called the Rodanthe Pier by locals and the Hatteras Island Fishing Pier by tourists. Fishermen come into the pier house, make their arrangements at the counter, and head out to the blackness of the pier itself.

"It was a whole resort—restaurant, 38-room motel, and 36 cottages," Cary explains. Hurricane Floyd knocked out the pier house in 1999, but the Hatteras Island Resort continued bringing visitors from out of state until 2003.

"Hurricane Isabel wiped that all out," Cary says. The pier itself, ironically, survived the storm. Ferocious waters churned around its pilings and over its decking but moved on without doing substantial harm. Nothing else was so lucky. The pier house was detached from the pier. The floor and the ocean-side wall of the restaurant were simply lifted out.

Rodanthe Pier owner T. J. Cary sees third- and fourth-generation visitors. He adds to the family atmosphere by giving rewards like fishing tackle and poles to students for good report cards.

Photograph by Vicki McAllister

Water went through the motel and lifted off its roof. The cottages suffered even more, being picked off their foundations and carried to destruction. All except a few. "We had remodeled five," Cary says. "Out of pure, stupid luck, the five we had just remodeled were the ones that survived." Those cottages have been moved elsewhere, the resort given up on, and much of the land sold. Now, the pier and pier house stand sentry. Even the parking lot often finds itself covered after a storm. This night, for instance, most of it is under sand.

Cary, born in 1954 and originally from Brooklyn, retired from his job in Virginia as a high-voltage electrician. He liked the family atmosphere of the pier. Cary adds to it, going so far as to ask children to show him their report cards, then rewarding them with everything from free tackle to fishing poles.

He knew the pier had a long history with visitors. "They've been coming in here since the '40s—third and fourth generations now." Cary points to an old picture of a handful of friends at the pier. The picture recently caught the eye of a visiting group. "This woman here," he says, indicating the figure in the middle, "it was her great-great-grandchildren who saw it."

C. E. Midgett, a marine in Vietnam and a lifelong fisherman, is in the pier house this night. He often is. He says it has always been "the number-one pier on the island. . . . People from everywhere come here. From China. They come out with 14-foot rods with bells on."

Thousands fish here each year. Large groups come in spring and summer. On a summer day, hundreds will be on the pier. "The fishing report controls a lot," Cary says. "The more they're catching, the busier it will be."

In spring, they might come to catch spot, sea mullet, puffer fish, cobia, bluefish, king mackerel, Spanish mackerel, and flounder. In June, it might be tarpon and croaker. August is the time for pompano, perhaps trout, maybe sheepshead around the pier pilings, along with trigger fish, black drum, even a few barracuda, and others. In fall, red drum—like Hooper's monster that remained a world-record catch until early this century—appear, along with striper and rockfish.

One fisherman, Chris Boyles, had a pair of unusual catches in the early 1980s at Rodanthe, courtesy of large storms.

The pier was still being rebuilt following one storm when "I caught a piling with my snag rig," Boyles says. Not exactly the easiest thing to reel in. The massive piece of treated lumber required all the power Boyles had, even with his industrial-strength fishing rig. Finally, he conquered the monster. "I got rewarded with a six-pack by the proprietors, who told me the going price per piling was about $1,500."

Boyles was out on the pier during a nor'easter another year and made an even more unusual catch—a one-pound, 10-ounce Maine lobster. "As news quickly spread of my unusual catch, the game warden greeted me on my way out of the pier house," Boyles remembers. The warden said he had to confiscate the lobster for a test. Boyles fretted he had run afoul of some regulation, but it turned out the warden had in mind a taste test. "I told him that I would make the test, and it turned out to be a good one. So I had my picture taken on that hallowed . . . catch board alongside the likes of Elvin Hooper and his then-world-record monster red and all the other immortal catches, me holding the itty-bitty lobster!"

The allure of the fishing pier is different things to different people, even at different times of year. "I love the summertime because there are so many different people," Cary says. "And in the wintertime, there's absolutely nobody here. You can see every light." He adds that, year-round, "the view's spectacular. It always changes. It never gets boring."

This pier has become a part of people's lives—and beyond. Cary says they gather on the pier after both weddings and funerals. As often as three times a year, someone will scatter the ashes of a relative off the end.

~

The walk up the ramp to the Avon Pier is steep. The pier house, built high off the beach, is not a typical one. The owner now is Ed Nunnally, a businessman from near Richmond, Virginia, who has made upgrades inside. The pier house is more finished than most, boasting a stylish gift and apparel shop that would be at home in a shopping mall.

But this is still Hatteras, and the pier house has the easy feel of the island. Woody Jones, behind the counter, has been on the island since 1998, when he retired at age 54 from a tire plant in Wilson. "All the towns, even Wilson, they get bigger and bigger," he says. "All the traffic, all the congestion." Again, the island is a counterpoint. The only rush hour comes in the summer months when tourists are around.

Ralph Crumpton, the fisherman sitting in the bag chair on the pier outside, worries more about the beach than he does the congestion. "This beach is eroding away," he says. He can give you the dates of some of the worst instances of erosion. He says old-timers blame the dune lines constructed on the island, which keep the sand from migrating north and south as it would. An inlet was cut into the island during Hurricane Isabel, he notes. A new one is trying to form at the northern edge of Rodanthe.

People talk about the hurricanes, but Crumpton says that "nor'easters down here are worse than hurricanes." The

Avon's striking pier house has a well-appointed gift and apparel shop that would be at home in a shopping mall. The exterior, not entirely subtle, leaves no doubt where you are.

Photograph by Vicki McAllister

winter storms, that is, are more damaging than their more famous fall brethren. "You get a hurricane, with winds from the southeast, it'll put sand *back* on the beach," he says. "A nor'easter won't."

Crumpton talks about the Avon Pier's soft curves and gentle rolls. The credit—or blame—for them is due the nor'easters. "The pier's sinking," he says. "The pilings are sinking." Nor'easters have been churning the waters around the pilings and digging out the base. Then, too, he adds, workmen over the years have made some uneven replacements. As for the fishing, "Avon's real shallow," he says. "Only five or six feet deep off the end of the pier at low tide. Rodanthe's about 30 feet." Big fish like cobia normally won't come that close to the shoals, he says.

Wayne Blessing leans against the railing of the Frisco Pier. He has been fishing the island since the piers opened. A former pilot in the United States Marines who even flew with baseball star Ted Williams during training in Pensacola, Florida, Blessing was enticed to Hatteras by a 1959 outdoor magazine article entitled, "The Day the Sea Ran Red." A "blitz" occurs when fish are so plentiful they appear to turn the water a different color. Indeed, Blessing speaks of seeing "so many channel bass out there, [the water] did turn red." Blessing first fished in Oregon Inlet in 1959—he caught a 35-pound channel bass on Thanksgiving weekend—and on the island itself in 1960, the year the bridge opened. By 1964, he bought a house in Frisco.

Most of his early fishing was in the surf, from the beach. "All the years that I fished, piers were the place you went if you didn't know how to fish," Blessing says, "which I found out isn't true." Fish are available from the piers that rarely are caught from the surf.

For half a century, fisherman Wayne Blessing has traveled from his home in Greensboro to the Hatteras surf and the Frisco Pier. "The challenge is a certain thrill that comes from feeling something on the line," he says. "I guess it's the same allure the gambler has."

Photograph by Vicki McAllister

Blessing learned the unwritten rules about the piers. "From what they tell me," he says, "each pier has its own culture. Some of the habitués are very protective. They don't want to see newcomers out on the pier."

For half a century, Blessing has made week-long or 10-day trips from his home in Greensboro, where he formerly worked in marketing for Proctor & Gamble, to his home in Frisco. The allure of Hatteras fishing? Blessing doesn't talk of days without deadlines. He doesn't talk of a life outdoors. He doesn't talk about the camaraderie of the pier people. None of that. "The challenge," he answers instead, is "a certain thrill that comes from feeling something on the line. I guess it's the same allure the gambler has."

Blessing has no idea how many fish he has caught, though he knows it's not as many as his late wife, Betty. She even caught what would have been a women's world record—a 22-pound bluefish—had she been using a different type of lure, he says proudly.

Blessing is one of a number of Frisco Pier regulars who calculate their stays in decades, rather than years. Jack Kepler, a relative newcomer by that standard, is sitting in a pier house chair. "I've been sitting here . . . for 20 years," he says. The claim is not quite literal. During a half-hour conversation, Kepler jumps up a dozen times to help customers and track down rods and point out photographs. But it does underscore the comfort he has with this place. Born in 1930, Kepler is from a small town in north-central Pennsylvania. He owned a profitable vending company, which rewarded his long hours with big profits. But this place was different. He could feel it.

Kepler came to Hatteras with his son. "I was 48 and on the fast track," he says. "As I say, 'When you finally learn what life's about, most of life is over.' " Before long, he and his wife built a home near the pier.

His wife's trips down are shorter, but Kepler usually remains much of the year, from April or May until Thanksgiving, before spending the winter months in tropical locations.

Kepler has learned about life here. "I learned how to fish and crab," he says, beginning a litany. "I understand time and nature better." The list is an amalgam of peculiarities that add up to a different understanding of things generally. By the time he reaches the end, he is smiling. "I learned another accent, a new language, even." He means the old Hatteras accent. "*Hoigh toider,*" he says as he gets up to answer the phone. Kepler tells the caller, "We're doing pretty good today. Caught a citation bass. Drum, mullet, even pompano." Pause. "Yes, pompano."

He returns. The water is 74 degrees today. When it drops to 68 degrees, he says, the serious fishermen will be

This vintage celebration of a barracuda catch was captured at the Cape Hatteras Fishing Pier, now known as the Frisco Pier. Surely, a million trophy pictures have been taken alongside the island's fishing piers. Fading Polaroids fill the bulletin boards of all three piers.

Photograph by Ray Couch, Outer Banks History Center

out. They arrive in October and again in the spring. They're after drum, sea mullet, pompano, yearling drum, flounder, speckled trout, gray trout, and the like.

Then there are the big fish—cobia, king mackerel, tarpon. Live bait is used. Two poles—an anchor pole and a fighting rod—are needed to haul in the really big ones. It can take a gaffe man running on the shore to help. "They're a special breed," Kepler says of the ones who go after the big fish. "They might sit out there all week and never get a bite." They don't give up, though. He walks over to the

Surf, sun, and old piers, like this one at Frisco, have been drawing those who fish to Hatteras for generations, even during the off-season. What could be better?

Photograph by Vicki McAllister

picture board, to the photos of a 78-pound tarpon, a 30-pound cobia, a 64-pound cobia, even a 75-pound cobia.

Two fishermen walk in. "They catching anything today?" one asks.

"Oh, yeah. Pompano. Caught a citation sea mullet," Kepler answers.

"Pompano, really?"

"Oh, yeah. . . . That's good eating."

"What did they use?"

"Shrimp, I think," Kepler says.

The Frisco Pier was built by several families, Kepler says. Ron Fuller, a member of the last of those families, sold it following Hurricane Isabel. The owner now is Todd Gaskill, whose wife, Angie, manages the pier. Todd Gaskill designed a machine to drive pier pilings into the ocean floor. Kepler says that's a handy machine to have on an island. It can take years to get replacement pilings after a storm, since those who do the work are mostly busy on the mainland. Gaskill replaced the 82 feet of pier lost to Isabel and added a T to the end.

Kepler has been ever-active since arriving on Hatteras, setting up companies for real estate, management, and marketing. He was part of the team behind the Hatteras by the Sea development. Still, he says, he has simplified his life, making a conscious effort to follow the rhythms of this place. That explains the pier. "I used to hang out here," he says. "They said I could work for $10 an hour a couple nights a week." The money is laughable compared to his take from other ventures.

Don't tell Kepler. He considers it a fortune.

Chapter Seventeen

HATTERAS VILLAGE

Katie Oden moved to the island in 1974. Raised in the Washington, D.C., area, she had lived in California and Florida as well. "I'd been living in California, and when I came back to Maryland, my friends had discovered Hatteras," she says. "In the fall of '73, I came down for a weekend. I came back in the spring of '74." She stayed.

The remote, storm-battered island convinced her to leave places many would consider more desirable. "The allure to me was the people," she says from behind the counter of her family's Sea Gull Motel in Hatteras Village. "It had the beautiful beaches and the woods, but it was the people."

She had been on the southern end of the island just a month, living with a girlfriend, when she was taken by surprise—at a cash register. "I went to the Red & White. I didn't have enough change," she remembers. She was about

The Burrus Red & White Supermarket in Hatteras Village, the oldest store on Hatteras Island, is still a gathering place. It was founded in 1866 as the Hatteras Store and Co. To the right is the historic 1901 weather station.

Photograph by
Vicki McAllister

Hatteras Island

to return the items. "They said, 'Oh, honey, just bring [the money] back tomorrow.' That doesn't happen." She was greeted warmly by the cashier when she repaid the money. "I was surprised she remembered my name."

The Burrus Red & White Supermarket is the oldest store on the island, founded in 1866 by a Union sympathizer who spent the Civil War in prison. After the war, he returned to Hatteras Island—where his father operated a gristmill—and opened the Hatteras Store and Co. Prosperity followed for the Stowe family, who operated the store, and the Burrus family, who married into it. "Instead of just staples like molasses, sugar, salt, flour, lard and so forth, we started getting some canned goods in and bottled drinks from Washington [North Carolina], New Bern and Elizabeth City by freight boat," the founder's grandson, W. Z. Burrus, recalled in a 1974 magazine article.

The original store was wooden, while the 1946 replacement is brick. But little else has changed. The store, located on the same spot in the heart of Hatteras, is still a community center. "This is the grocery store to go to if you're vacationing in Hatteras," one online forum says. "We have been traveling to Hatteras for over 30 years and this grocery store has not changed." Elsewhere, that might mean a store is out of date, insufficient, an anachronism. On Hatteras, it means the store is just right.

Hatteras Village sometimes seems a contradiction. Tourism dollars drive the local economy, and fine restaurants and pricey homes have come along for the ride. Set in part around a harbor, though, the village has a different feel, a different ambiance, a different raison d'être, than the rest of the island. This once was the quintessential fishing village. Fishing was all there was—that and working at the Durants Life-Saving Station (originally the Hatteras Life-Saving Station) or the Coast Guard station that followed.

The village still has a handful of marinas, a charter fishing industry, and the soul of a fishing village. Thank Hatteras Inlet for that. Hatteras Village had been intermittently connected to Ocracoke Island, but the 1846 hurricane severed them for good. Because of the new inlet, Hatteras was suddenly important, the connector between the ocean and Pamlico Sound. In 1858, it received the island's first post office. Indeed, it is the only village on the island not to see its name change after receiving a post office.

By 1896, Hatteras was a thriving village with 500 residents, four stores, and five boatbuilders. It would prosper in other ways. The 1870 census had shown that 50 percent of islanders were illiterate, on par with the rest of the state. But a village school opened at the turn of the 20th century. By 1920, the illiteracy rate in Hatteras Village was down to 16 percent.

The first car on the island showed up in Hatteras Village in 1918, an Avon old-timer remembered years later. "A man to Hatteras had it, Ellsworth Burrus," he said. "And he come up here on Sunday and takes out people for fifty cent a head to ride in it. That was like an airplane then."

A so-called porpoise fishery, actually designed for bottle-nosed dolphins, was based in the village from the late 1800s until 1926. Working it was not for the faint of heart. Dolphins, caught with large nets controlled by four boats, were hooked in the blowhole and dragged to shore. Beached overnight, they were left gasping before being butchered the next morning in a brutal process that first saw them stabbed in the heart under the left fin. Their death squeals were so loud and distressing that they frightened nearby horses. But there was good money in the business. After each dolphin was killed, its hide was removed, as was its lower jawbone, from which oil was taken that brought $1,000 a barrel. The butchered dolphins were then taken to the

Hatteras Village, shown in an undated photograph from the middle of the last century, was the focal point of the island's commerce from the mid-1800s, when Hatteras Inlet was opened in a storm, for more than a century until Highway 12 was built. Still an important locale for tourism, commercial fishing, and charter fishing, it is the home of a maritime museum, a weather museum, and a Coast Guard station.

Aycock Brown Collection, Outer Banks History Center

The A. S. Austin Store was an island favorite for the first half of the 20th century. During the 1930s, children would buy candy and soft drinks, then go next door to a movie house run by Ander Austin's son, Shanklin.

Aycock Brown Collection, Outer Banks History Center

processing factory to have further oil removed.

Commercial fishing has been a Hatteras Village livelihood almost from the beginning, though the percentage of residents involved has steadily fallen. Sixty percent of Hatteras men fished in 1870. By 1950, the percentage dropped to 23, though the village still had 40 fishing boats and several fish-packing houses.

The earliest fish-packing houses, built before the harbor was dug, were situated a couple hundred yards out into the

The island's largest commercial fishing industry was in Hatteras, and fish-packing houses were a key component. Before the harbor was dug, fish houses were situated out in Pamlico Sound.

Charter boats and other fishing and recreational vessels line the picturesque harbor at Hatteras. On the opposite page, the 75-foot Miss Hatteras charter boat waits in the harbor outside the Breakwater Restaurant for its next excursion.

Photographs by
Vicki McAllister

sound. Footbridges connected a few to the shore. Eventually, driving ramps were built out to them, though that could present difficulties. "My uncle was the first one to build a pier to his fish house that you could drive on," one villager remembered. "My cousin, Vern, he run off of it. The steering on some of the old Model A's wasn't as good. Lot of loose motion."

Ephriam O'Neal, born in 1920, said in a 2006 interview with the North Carolina Fisheries Association that, "when I was a boy, there were at least seven fish houses here in the village. . . . Mr. John Meekins had a fish house down where Lee Robinson's store is. It had a long pier that was about six feet wide and probably ran 400 yards out into the sound where the water was five or six feet deep." Other fish houses were owned by Deck Oden, Roscoe Burrus, Twine Willis, Irish Willis, Dan Oden, and Ander Austin.

The 1936 hurricane took down most of them, O'Neal said. "Oh, I remember that storm well. I was standing inside and the water was up to my belt. It washed the house off its blocks." After that hurricane and the dredging of the harbor, fish houses were built inside the harbor.

As elsewhere on the island, general stores were gathering spots. The Burrus store, though the first, was far from the only one in Hatteras Village. Lee Robinson's general store, begun in 1948, continues today. Before that, Ander Austin ran a store for much of the first half of the 20th century; boys bought fishhooks five for a penny at the A. S. Austin Store. Beginning in the 1930s, children first stopped for candy and drinks, then went next door to the movie house run by Ander's son, Shanklin Austin. Admission to a movie was 25 cents. For 10 cents, they could get a bag of salted Planters peanuts and a Pepsi; they mixed the two and shook them up. The theater closed when Shanklin was called to duty in World War II.

The island's weather station was another important spot. Housed at the lighthouse keepers' quarters in Buxton for its first six years, it was moved to the Durants Life-Saving Station at Hatteras in 1880, then to a private residence in 1883. In 1901, it got a building of its own, near the Burrus store.

"It was one of 12 stations built at the turn of the [20th] century," says National Park Service ranger Mark Theune, who gives tours. "Only two have been restored." The weather station was moved back to the cape after World War II. This Hatteras building, recently restored to its original green-and-yellow color scheme, now houses a visitor center and weather museum. Weekly tours are offered during the tourist season.

The weather station was not an immediate hit with the locals, Theune says. "The meteorologist hated the job. The community hated the weather bureau." Suspicious Hatteras residents thought the weather installation was up to no good, he says. They believed the government wanted "outside infiltrators."

Moreover, it was not an easy job. Turn-of-the-20th-century weather forecasting and recordkeeping were done manually. An officer or an assistant took hourly recordings of temperature, humidity, wind velocity, solar radiation, precipitation, and pressure, recording them in a logbook. No matter what the weather was, readings had to be taken.

Through the years, the weather officers also launched weather balloons with measurement-transmitting radiosonde boxes, perused the skies and seas from a small observation deck atop the second story, and raised appropriate warning flags—the only available forecasts, which the villagers sometimes ignored. Celeste Strom, a park service ranger, says simply, "Locals were hard to get off [the island] during hurricanes."

The station was also important in the development of

The historic Hatteras weather station, shown here circa 1901–9, was the first to receive the distress signal of the Titanic when it struck an iceberg in 1914. The station, added to the National Register of Historic Places in 1978, today is a weather museum and visitor center.

Photographs by H. H. Brimley, North Carolina State Archives (left), and Vicki McAllister (opposite)

forecasting techniques, thanks to the changing and challenging weather of Hatteras. It came to have historic value as well, because of the reception of the *Titanic*'s distress call in 1914, eerily recorded in the typewritten logbook: "He says 'Have struck iceberg.' " The building has been on the National Register of Historic Places since 1978.

As the village grew, so did opportunities.

From the 1930s until the 1960s, women ages 18 to 28 could belong to the Girl's Club, started by New Jersey industrialist George A. Lyons. It was a hot spot for its table tennis, cards, and checkers. Perhaps a bigger allure was that members could shower after going into the ocean.

Square dances held at the Atlantic View Hotel Pavilion, the Beacon, and Horton's were popular until the 1950s, though fights broke out occasionally with visitors from other villages, particularly Rodanthe.

Captain Ernal Foster began the charter fishing business at Hatteras in 1937, starting the famed Albatross Fleet. It got a boost when big-city outdoors columnists began writing about the great fishing they had enjoyed off Hatteras with him. The industry grew rapidly in the 1950s with the advent of marlin fishing. Foster himself caught a 475-pound marlin in 1951. A decade later, he caught a world-record 810-pounder.

Since the introduction of tourism and the building of an island-long highway, an interesting dynamic has been at play on Hatteras Island. Businesses on the northern end, by and large, do better than those on the southern end.

The reason is simple: distance. Hatteras Village is the southernmost spot on the 50-mile-long island, or at least the southernmost spot with a road. It is an hour's drive or so from the islandopolis of Roanoke Island. While the inlet once made Hatteras the most accessible of island villages, the highway now makes it the least. Those wanting the

The Atlantic View Hotel, built in Hatteras Village in the 1920s, was the island's first true hotel. The second, the Avon Hotel, was not constructed until 1952.

Aycock Brown Collection, Outer Banks History Center

Hatteras Island experience need drive only to the Tri-Village to find it. A little farther and they can visit Avon and Buxton—and Buxton, of course, is the home of the world-famous lighthouse. Why go farther?

"It's that lighthouse," says Katie Oden, behind the desk of the Sea Gull Motel. "First-timers, they get to Buxton and they think they're there. They don't realize the island turns and there's more."

The Sea Gull had an advantage for a while. "We were one of the few Triple-A motels on the island," Oden says, referring to being listed in the American Automobile Association's oft-used tour books. "We were listed under *Hatteras*. We were the only ones who were Triple-A approved in Hatteras." Other motels on the island were listed under

Katie Oden, shown outside her office at the Sea Gull, first saw Hatteras Island in 1973, came back the next spring, and stayed. "The allure to me was the people," she says. "It had the beautiful beaches and the woods, but it was the people."

Photograph by Vicki McAllister

The Sea Gull Motel, shown here in a postcard from the 1960s, was built in the 1950s. Hurricane Isabel destroyed most of it in 2003, trapping young Marci Oden in the motel and then sweeping her into a garage. She stayed in an attic until rescued. Her parents, the motel's owners, renovated the two-story building at the far end of the complex. The rest of the motel was destroyed.

Author's collection

Buxton, which meant little to first-timers looking for accommodations on Hatteras Island. That advantage is gone now that the listings are under *Outer Banks*.

After the devastation of Hurricane Isabel in 2003, the Odens weren't sure they wanted back in the business anyway. "Isabel knocked down the whole hotel," Katie Oden says. "This was the original building. . . . It had at least three feet of sand in it." The family's decision was an economic one. "We weren't going to rebuild. We didn't want to go back to 45 rooms. . . . Before Isabel, we had 45 rooms and weren't full all summer."

There was a history, however. Though Katie Oden arrived only in the 1970s, her husband's family was one of the early ones on the island, and the Oden name, like a handful of others, can be seen throughout the village. The Oden family built the Sea Gull in the early 1950s as a seven-room building before constructing apartments and an office and adding a second story to the original structure.

Finally, after Isabel, they decided to just refurbish the original two-story building. "Right now, 15 rooms is more than we need with the economy," Oden says. Regular customers are glad. Some of the same visitors have been coming to the Sea Gull Motel for 15 or 20 years. A few, far longer.

This, after all, is a village and an island where time seems measured not so much in hours or days. It is measured in generations.

Chapter Eighteen

THIS HATTERAS LIFE

"People have the perception of being at the end of the earth—you know, the *Outer* Banks," Danny Couch says. He is sitting in a conference room at Hatteras Realty in Avon.

In a certain sense, Hatteras *is* the end of the earth, or at least the end of the continent, sticking out almost too far into a treacherous sea, punished by wind and rain and cold.

Couch is among the many who would be nowhere else. His father moved to the island from Chapel Hill in 1963, buying a filling station and tackle shop in Buxton from a man shaken by the infamous Ash Wednesday Storm the previous year. Young Danny was just three years old, and the island was already a part of him. He remembers being stirred by its history when he read parts of David Stick's *Graveyard of the Atlantic*—not exactly a comic book—as a seven-year-old second-grader.

Couch has interviewed more than 300 old-timers about the island, going back to his high-school days at Cape Hatteras School, when he worked for the *Sea Chest*. The quarterly magazine, in existence from 1973 through the mid-1990s (with the exception of a few years in the middle), is a treasure trove of information about fishing methods, traditional healing practices, and other cultural and historical topics. The first issue featured an interview with Maurice Bernard "Doc" Folb, the navy's chief pharmacist's mate, who worked out of the radio station in Buxton, serving eight Coast Guard stations and five lighthouses. Folb, whose predecessor died in the flu epidemic of 1919, also treated residents up and down the island and set up a small nursing school in each village. One of Couch's favorite stories came from Dewey Basnett of Trent, who told how the first two cars on the island collided head-on the first time they got near each other.

Couch, too, is a treasure trove. An interview with him traverses centuries, going forward and backward, tying together seemingly unrelated events, from sea currents to the Battle of Hatteras to fishing to storms to automobiles. The connectivity is astounding. Couch revels in the intricacies of Hatteras, the permutations, the nooks and crannies. All of it figures into the Hatteras life, as evinced by just a few points he offers:

⚓ "Old-time sailors would look for porpoises and whales" to show them the deepwater routes through Diamond Shoals, he says.

⚓ In 1532, Verrazano saw Cape Woods, now Buxton Woods, and sent a boat ashore to get water. But earlier explorers had passed by. "Our Indians saw the sails out there," he says. "It must have been like looking at Martians."

⚓ The Gulf Stream flows north at four to six miles an hour. Though Hatteras interrupted its flow, it was once a major

Danny Couch, island tour operator and historian when he's not a real-estate agent, was stirred by Hatteras history as early as the second grade by reading from David Stick's Graveyard of the Atlantic. *Shown here at the Chicamacomico Life-Saving Station, Couch has interviewed more than 300 old-timers, collecting a treasure trove of stories.*

Photograph by Vicki McAllister

highway, the interstate of its time. "One hundred, 200, 400 years ago, I-95 was that way," he says, gesturing toward the east, "in the ocean."

"Ben Dixon MacNeill, he put a lot of crap out there," Couch says. One such story concerned the family of Richard Dailey, the man who picked up the first distress call from the *Titanic* in 1912. According to Couch, writer MacNeill claimed that "Dailey's great-grandfather washed up on the island. . . . Ben Dixon MacNeill [also] made up the story about *Thunderbolt*," a ship he said nearly wrecked during a Hatteras storm while carrying the young Alexander Hamilton.

Seven of the most inventive minds of the age either worked on or visited the Outer Banks around the turn of the 20th century: the Wright brothers, Reginald Fessenden, Guglielmo Marconi, Lee De Forest, Thomas Edison, and—this may be stretching things—Thomas Edison, Jr.

Sixty-two percent of the island belongs to either the National Park Service or the United States Fish and Wildlife Service. Another 9 percent belongs to state and local governments. Another 8 percent, though privately owned, is wetlands. That leaves just 21 percent for building.

The Cape Hatteras School, opened in 2008, cost more than $22 million for just 151 middle- and high-school students.

Movie stars Tom Hanks, Richard Gere, and Kevin Costner have been frequent visitors to the island.

Football star Dan Marino and hockey star Mark Messier bought homes in Hatteras Landing.

Build here and you'd better enjoy living here. "There's a myth that these houses pay for themselves" with rental income, he says. "They don't."

Joe Schwarzer, director of the Graveyard of the Atlantic Museum, has an apt description for the natives' reaction to the many shipwrecks and the goods that washed ashore over the years. "Joe said, 'When ships came ashore, it was like having a Walmart wash up,' " Couch relates.

Hatteras means, loosely, "there is less vegetation." A professor at UNC-Pembroke says Chicamacomico means "the land of sinking-down sand."

The Oden family can trace its ancestry to a shipwreck in 1859.

"We do have a big drug problem," Couch says. Otherwise, "we have very little crime."

☀ Contrary to what is related in *The Lost Colony*, the popular, long-running play in Manteo, ample evidence exists that the colonists went to Hatteras Island. "[Hatteras native] Dale Burrus said the Lost Colony was never lost until they started that pageant," Couch says.

☀ "People come down here and know they can go barefoot the rest of their life," he says.

And on it goes. Couch could talk for hours about Hatteras. He often does, offering at least eight excursions aboard his Hatteras Tours bus, including full-island tours of Hatteras, Ocracoke, and Roanoke islands, plus smaller specialty tours centered on Kinnakeet, the Civil War, and ghosts. In fact, give him a topic and a few people to drive around the island and Couch will lead a tour.

Many come here because of the outdoors. Stop by Pamlico Bay in Rodanthe most days and you'll find kite boarders. When a breeze is blowing, the sky is full of surfers held aloft by brightly colored chutes, navigating their way on waves of air. It is a surreal sight—something out of a dream, colorful, floating.

Among the many here this afternoon are Brian Walters and Chris Decle, members of the Florida State Kiteboard Association, who made the trip northward just for Hatteras.

Kite boarding, not much more than a decade old, is the world's fastest-growing sport, Decle says, and "Hatteras is one of the number-one places. . . . Because Hatteras is such a long, skinny island, with a long coastline," circumstances are almost ideal. Cold winds from the northeast meet warmer winds out of the southwest. The resulting breezes are consistent, Decle says. The rough waters of the Atlantic

Hatteras Island

No one comes to Hatteras without expecting to spend a good part of their time outdoors. But recreation—indeed, everyday life—on the island is always subject to the whims of weather and surf. Even the warped and seemingly tenuous fishing piers, like this one at Avon, show the effects of nature.

Photograph by Vicki McAllister

allow for spirited rides. The smooth waters of the sound allow for tricks.

Larry and Susan Russ agree that the shallow, flat waters of the sound make for perfect kite boarding. It is why they've come here this summer—all the way from Oregon.

A cousin to kite boarding is windsurfing. A popular site for windsurfing is Canadian Hole, south of Avon, so named for its influx of Canadian visitors. Old-timers know the spot as "the haulover," a narrow part of the island where wooden boats once were hauled from the sound to the ocean.

The almost mind-boggling array of outdoor activities on Hatteras includes surfing, biking, walking, sailing, boating, paddleboating, water-skiing, Jet Skiing, swimming, diving, snorkeling, paragliding, fishing (surf fishing, pier fishing, deep-sea fishing, sound and bay fishing), sightseeing, beachcombing, whale and dolphin watching, bird-watching, and even ecotourism. And that doesn't include visiting amusement parks and the like.

Many engage in swimming and sunbathing. Everyone swims in the ocean—it is an essential part of Hatteras life—but frankly, better places exist. The Hatteras waves and currents are legendary for their treachery. Rudy Gray, who managed the Hatteras Island Fishing Pier from 1961 to 1982, several times had to save drowning swimmers, as have many a Coast Guardsman and lifeguard. Gray particularly remembers one man who got caught in a rip current and was taken into the ocean alongside the pier:

> I heard this hollering that someone was on the beach drowning. I just kind of ran out the pier door, and when I ran out the pier door I could see this man out there, and he was not any distance from the pier. He got into what we call one of the "outlets" there, and it took him out. He was just really about to give out. So just dear old me, I just jumped off the pier, dove off the pier into the ocean.

We used to do it all the time. . . . So I dove over, swam down there to him, got up there to him, rescued him, and pulled him.

Surfing has been popular on Hatteras longer than many might expect, going back to the 1950s. Leslie Hooper and Gaskill Austin had the jump on the rest of the world. The two boys gathered up old planks from shipwrecks—dunnage—and used them as boards. But surfing was not without its dangers, as Austin recalled years later:

One day, I got too far out on a wave and curled, and the board dipped in the sand, rode me up over it, and I slid off. A piece of the board split off the size of my finger [and] went up through my armpit and came out through the back of my shoulder. I got stabbed good. My uncle held me down and put his foot on my shoulder and arm and yanked the thing out, and I went back in the ocean in the salt water and soaked in the salt water. Then I came home and hid [the wound] for a week or two until it healed up.

Boards now are safer, made of hard foam covered by fiberglass, cloth, and an epoxy.

Laura Heitsenrether has been coming to Hatteras since the late 1980s, when she was just four or five. "I'm from New Jersey and grew up at the beach—Ocean City." It, too, is a barrier island, but far more crowded than Hatteras. Her family began visiting here every Easter week. Her father and brother surfed, and she started as well.

Heitsenrether fell in love with the island and continued coming down during college. After graduating, she got her real-estate license and went to work in New Jersey, already on a career track to early success. But while she was planning another trip to Hatteras, lining up her rental property, she saw a listing of careers at the bottom of the page.

Perhaps nowhere on the East Coast are outdoor watersports more a part of the culture than at Hatteras. Wind and waves combine for spectacular thrills in kite boarding, surfing and windsurfing.

Photographs by Vicki McAllister

"I thought, 'Oh, my god, why don't I?'"

So she did. Heitsenrether moved to Hatteras Island, giving up the life she thought she had been working toward. "I'm renting, staying in a trailer," she says now, laughing. Her enthusiasm picks up as she describes the incongruity of it all. "I went from a two-bedroom condo in New Jersey to a trailer in Avon. And I'm so much happier. It's great. I can walk to work, ride my bicycle to the store."

The difference in culture, in attitude, is striking. "In New Jersey, it was all about money. In real estate, it was all about the next deal, making the deal. It was all about what you have, where you live. In New Jersey, if you live in a trailer, that's . . ." She breaks off the sentence, laughing. Living in a trailer would be unthinkable. It would be failure, pure and simple.

On Hatteras, it's living. "Every morning, I ride my bike down to the beach and surf from 6 to 8 A.M." Then it's off to work at a realty office. "Then I'll surf from 6 to 8 P.M., at least on a good day." Laura Heitsenrether has found lots of friends, though she says many more males than females live on the island.

Trade-offs are necessary for this Hatteras life, of course. "When I tell people I've moved down here, they say, 'Wait till winter.' The restaurants are closed. The gas stations close at 7 P.M. A lot of people down here, they collect unemployment." In the town of Avon, she says, only a couple of realty companies, a hardware store, and a grocery store brave the winters.

Ah, the Hatteras winters.

It is in winter, perhaps, that Hatteras is most as it used to be. The island has a large summer population—indeed, Cape Hatteras National Seashore receives about 3 million visitors a year. But the island's permanent residents—the ones who stick it out through the winter—number only about 3,000 or 4,000. The island can seem empty.

"In January, I have my birthday and my anniversary, and there's never a restaurant that stays open," Katie Oden says, expressing what is a minor lament for a year-rounder. Not everyone wants to brave the winters. "I've got several sisters," she says. "They would come down every year. They really love it. But of all my family, I don't know of any who would live here year-round."

Oden says the winter is more than okay by her, however. "I love it. There's more time for friends." The pace is slower. Finally, the family has time for everything. "We refresh in the winter."

"In December and January," says Woody Jones, who retired to the island in 1998, "I drive the beach and don't see a soul for three or four miles." He doesn't mean a few people. He means no people. He doesn't mean occasionally. He means routinely.

When fisherman Ralph Crumpton started visiting Hatteras in the early 1960s, all he found were small cottages. Small cottages and the new pier at Avon, his home base. Now, there's considerably more. So it's not surprising that Crumpton is one of those islanders who love Hatteras in the winter, too. "This is a good place to come in the winter," he insists. "You can get away from everything. No people. No noise."

Crumpton even finds a silver lining in the island's development. Winter storms used to knock out electricity to the sparsely populated island for spans of two to three weeks. Now, islanders usually have power restored in two or three days.

Irene Nolan says flatly, "The winter is the best time. No one's here."

Nolan is a newswoman who chose this place. She knows why others do, too. The former managing editor of the

Louisville Courier-Journal visited for years before she moved here. She then spent 16 years as editor of the *Island Breeze*. She now edits the online paper www.IslandFreePress.org, a must-read that combines aggressive reporting on issues like beach access with island news and historical pieces such as Buddy Swain's "Precious Memories" series.

"I came here in '75 with my children, to Nags Head," Nolan says. She found herself driving south. "Every single day for a week, I drove to Hatteras—an hour—because I had never seen a more beautiful beach. . . . The allure was not only how beautiful it was but how undeveloped it was. The fact that the park service did come here and set up the park made it different than Nags Head and Kill Devil Hills."

Nolan says those who move to Hatteras, as she ended up doing, don't always get what they expect. "Some people love the life here, and some people don't," she says. Always, there are forces pushing people off the island. "Some people can't stand the winter, and they leave. Some people can't stand the storms, and they leave."

The island and its lifestyle attract talented people—artists, Ph.D.s, lawyers, and the like. They have to work at staying, Nolan says. "If you're on the outside looking in, it looks very laid-back. If you're living it, you'll see people working three jobs in the summer."

She says that "people don't come here for the nightlife, the music. There is none." But some don't realize how truly quiet Hatteras becomes in winter. "They're absolutely taken with it on vacation. This is where they want to live. They think they can make it with lesser jobs. I know people with Ph.D.s who clean up houses on the weekend. A lot think they can do that. [But] it is very isolated, especially in winter."

Always, the specter of storms hangs over the island. "Hurricanes are a challenge for a lot of people," Nolan says.

The first one she experienced was Emily in 1993, two years after she and her husband moved to the island. "About the time the water got over the fence, I said to [my husband], 'Does the water usually get up our fence?' " It kept rising. She noticed another oddity. "I said, 'Look at all those ducks out on the street.' He said, 'Those aren't ducks, those are my decoys.' "

In 1999, when Nolan's husband was undergoing bypass surgery off the island, Hurricane Dennis tore out the highway between Avon and Buxton. In 2003, Isabel cut an inlet above Hatteras Village. The cleanup work after Isabel was immense. "That's when you get the feeling of what brings people together."

Nolan loves the island even in winter. "It's a real small-town atmosphere. People look out for their neighbors. Everyone gets along." They had better. "The gossip mill is relentless," she adds.

At its core, then, what is the Hatteras life? What is its hold over so many people? Is it the open spaces? The storms? The sense of independence?

Danny Couch, who may know as much of the island as anyone, considers. "It's the people," he answers. "To go sit on a porch, drinking tea, using a rolled-up newspaper to swat the flies, *watching* the flies."

Later, after a dozen conversational detours, Couch returns to the topic, as if confirming it to himself. "It is the people," he says, giving a slight nod. "It is home." He pauses, thinking. "Some of my best memories are going out on the beach with my father in an open Jeep. . . . It's the people."

Chapter Nineteen

HATTERAS TOMORROW

Through luck, design, and nature's death grip, Hatteras Island continues to remain free of some of the excesses of unbridled growth.

But hardly all.

A fisherman laments the changes. "The money is what makes things go," he says. "Most of the growth is outside developers coming in. . . . [They] could care less about the island. All they are interested in is money. Build it and go."

Gee Gee Rosell, the owner of Buxton Village Books, says flatly, "I don't recognize it anymore. It's changed so much since I got here." Roselle finds the turning point easy to identify. "The atmosphere changed when Hatteras Island began to be seen as a lucrative real-estate investment," she says. "And what boggles my mind is, we're 30 miles out to sea. The road is closed regularly by storms." The growth started in the 1980s and exploded the following decade, she says. Massive investment homes—so-called LLCs, or limited liability companies, the type of business setups often used—have indirectly driven up the cost of living and nearly overpowered the local infrastructure. "They're nobody's beloved second home," Rosell says. That's what she finds most galling.

Irene Nolan, editor of the online paper www.Island FreePress.org, says tourism and development have changed "the feeling of the island a little bit." But they have also made possible a better road, improved medical care, and the like. On the whole, tourism is a mixed blessing. "It brought prosperity to a lot of people," she says. "It also brought headaches to a lot of people." For a long time, fishermen and families came to Hatteras, Nolan says. Now, visitors are as likely to be "the young party crowd who are ill-behaved and upscale people who want amenities."

The 21st-century real-estate boom is evident to both those looking to buy and those looking to sell. A Buxton man who inherited land from his father says he sold it for $30,000 to $40,000 an acre in 1992. A decade later, he was selling it for $100,000 to $150,000.

Ernal Foster was the famed founder of the Albatross Fleet of charter fishing boats and, in essence, the charter boat fishing industry in Hatteras Village. His son Ernie, a teacher and fisherman who took over the fleet, wrote a guest column for the Nolan-edited *Island Breeze* in 2002 during a fight over a large development in his home village. It remains one of the most-read pieces on the "new" Hatteras. Entitled "Thoughts on Watching a Village Die," Ernie Foster's piece says in part,

> The place where I grew up was magical. It was a small place (population 500) where everyone knew everyone. It was a place where everyone seemed to be self sufficient (a common trait among fishermen). And it was a place where everyone seemed to want to help each other. . . .
>
> Contrast this with what is happening today. The village itself is literally under assault. A place where people

Old and new intermingle on Hatteras. The old, like this one-story cottage, tends to be small and understated. The new, like this adjacent three-story cottage, often seems grafted onto the island, almost of a different type entirely.

Photograph by Vicki McAllister

lived, worked, and raised families for centuries is converted into a mass of nondescript "rental machines." . . .

Make no mistake! These projects and countless other structures being built are not an attempt to improve the village. . . . These are outside, short-term investors who will change forever the physical nature of the village and its social fabric. Once these structures are built, they will be there beyond our lifetime. . . .

This is how Hatteras village will die one monster structure at a time, 55 feet in the air, built to be sold immediately to the next buyer who plans to do the same with no interest in the life and well being of Hatteras as a viable community.

It is a common theme on the island.

An Avon old-timer worries that the culture of the village is eroding. "People are going into Avon and paying a half-million dollars for those old houses and tearing them down. They're putting up places on stilts. Once the old people are gone, it's over."

Meanwhile, Jack Kepler, the Pennsylvania businessman who moved down to spend half his life sitting in a chair on the Avon Pier, sees visitors unconsciously damaging what lured them in the first place. "People from New Jersey, they fall in love with this place, they come down here, and they build those mini-motels," he says, frustrated by the irony. "Then they wonder, 'What happened to that little beach house with the screened-in porch with holes in the screen?' "

The same question is asked every generation, every decade, sometimes every year. In her 1987 work, *Hatteras Journal*, Jan DeBlieu talked with Old Christmas attendee

Hatteras Island's most striking structure, without a doubt, remains the Cape Hatteras Lighthouse. The second most striking? It now may be this large, bright yellow T-shirt and souvenir shop in Avon. The shop opened in 2008.

Photograph by Vicki McAllister

Joyce Rucker, whose family had been participating for generations: "We wouldn't miss it for the world," Rucker said. "This is still home in some ways. But my, it's changed. Every year there are more strangers. There's no way to stop more people from coming here. The island's growing, and in many ways it's good that we have the kinds of amenities we have now. It was hard to live the way we did, with no electricity or roads. We have a movie theater in Avon. I never thought I would live to see a movie theater open in Avon."

Avon has a good deal more than a movie theater now, of course.

A lifelong Avon man laments the tenor of the changes, citing a brief incident that occurred on the shore of Pamlico Sound:

> All my life, people have taken their families one particular place. They've worked in the water, they've put up their umbrellas, they take their boats in and out. But the land has been sold to people from New England or from Florida. [An Avon] family sat down on the sandy beach and looked out towards the sound. Pretty soon, this person approached them and said, "You people are on my land." She was absolutely right in what she owned legally, but do you see the change that has come about? Who would suspect that anybody in Avon would ever say, "Hey, you're trespassing on my land"?

Fishermen—particularly commercial fishermen—see their way of life disappearing. Ignatius "I. D." Midgett said it will be lost in part because of overregulation. "I think a way of life is going to be lost, if nothing else," he lamented in a park service interview. "A heritage is going to be lost. Like the cowboy—he's gone—so the fishermen are going to be gone, too. Farmers are always having a hard

Commercial fishermen complain they are being squeezed out of what has been for generations both their families' heritage and the most important industry on Hatteras. This photo shows fishermen working their nets during a historic run of gray trout in 1974.

Photograph by Ray Couch, Outer Banks History Center

time. Farmers and fishermen always had a hard time. The only thing the farmer does is get a little help. The fisherman doesn't. The farmer gets subsidized. The fisherman doesn't get anything except hard time."

Not just the Hatteras way of life is under attack. The island itself is continually buffeted by nature, a force more potent than even developers.

Barrier islands are never static. Winds and waves drive the sands, reshaping them, cutting them apart, putting them back together elsewhere, even picking them up and moving them. Geologists estimate that the Outer Banks have moved three to five feet to the west every year for the last century. The shoreline at the lighthouse is the most noted section, but movement is routine up and down the coast. North of Cape Hatteras, the shoreline averages five feet of migration to the south and west a year. At Oregon Inlet, the pace is 15 feet a year, and the inlet itself is moving nearly 100 feet per year. Since it opened in the storm of 1846, Oregon Inlet has moved more than two miles south and a third of a mile west. The Bonner Bridge already is spanning sand at its northern end.

Man has taken a stab at affecting the equation, too. Gabriel Francis Lee, in a 2008 master's thesis for North Carolina State University, explains the dynamic:

> [Highway] 12 became the economic lifeline of the postwar Outer Banks. That road, and that relationship, was built on the foundation of natural barrier island stability assumed by scientists since the turn of the 20th century. In the early 1970s, that foundation quickly eroded.
>
> New science proved definitively that barrier islands were inherently migratory landscapes that rolled landward with the rising sea. The shoreline erosion that conservationists thought they were preventing was actually sand displacement, a normal and necessary function of

Barrier islands are meant to shift with the wind and currents. However, once homes and rental properties are erected—or a lighthouse—the temptation is to try to keep the beach in place. The job becomes ever more difficult and expensive—and never a permanent fix, as shown by these exposed sandbags from a federal shoreline control project in the early 1970s. A series of destructive nor'easters followed that work, and the project was abandoned. The National Park Service soon after adopted its current "let nature take its course" policy. That brought to an end federal beach maintenance begun four decades earlier (though with a halt for World War II).

Photograph by Vicki McAllister

barrier island systems. The findings, furthermore, showed that any shoreline stabilizing structure, even soft structures like dunes, actually accelerates rates of beach loss. To continue the current policy meant courting future disaster. To fulfill their mandate of preserving the islands in their natural state, the Park Service relinquished dune maintenance in the mid-1970s. But instead of creating radically new relationships with the land that would allow the islands to move, management of the shore largely transferred to the North Carolina Department of Transportation which continued to construct dunes in the interest of protecting the road, and thus property and access. Because stabilized shoreline structures destroy beaches, supporting dune maintenance forced the state to endorse a policy of "beach nourishment," pumping dredging sand from the ocean bottom onto the shore and spreading it with bulldozers to form new beaches. Faced with the option of protecting property or protecting beaches, the state decided that, at great cost, they would do both. Over the last half of the 20th century, public dollars continually re-created "natural" space and maintained access to it on the Outer Banks.

A Salvo resident complains about how flooding following hurricanes is made worse by dunes: "You get that surge because of northeast winds pushing water through the inlets into the sound. [After the storm's eye passes,] you get a sudden shift of wind, and that water tries to come back at once. It's taken days to get there. [The dunes] block the water from going back into the ocean, and we get floods."

The resident puts it bluntly: "The dunes protect the houses of the people who don't have any more brains than to build right on the ocean."

Some will always complain about intrusions into the island and its spirit—and with good reason. Still, few places have better adapted to keeping their souls alive in the face of economic assault than Hatteras.

Fishermen have come to the Frisco Pier for generations. Only recently have they looked back on the shoreline to see large rental homes—dubbed "mini-hotels" or "McMansions"—going up. The Hatteras building boom, though almost minis-cule compared to that of many island resorts, has affected most of the villages.

Photograph by Vicki McAllister

A Buxton resident says recent tourism growth has been a positive: "Nice families come surfing today. In the beginning, it was beach bums, hippies. They just wrecked houses and stole. They would sleep on the beach and go sneak under the houses that were rented."

A Frisco man says that tourism and development, however overpowering, have provided employment and allowed villagers to stay on the island. "I'm almost afraid we're going too far with overbuilding," he admits. "A lot of people cuss it, but at the same daggone time, where would we be without it? You've got to take the bitter with the sweet." Ironically, island transplants complain most about growth and tourism, he says. "They come in from the outside and don't know what it was like before tourism got here."

Most of the island remains untouched—or minimally touched, at least—by man. Federal oversight protects most of the fragile island from development. Mother Nature takes care of much of the more foolish development that is allowed.

Hatteras remains a storm-battered island of sun and sand, of wind and wave, of history and tomorrow. Sea gulls fly overhead. Mullet swim below. Dolphins and egrets are there for those who look. Shipwrecks, lifesaving stations, and even tiny post offices lend character. The waves, the beach, the dunes, the marshes, and the woods belong to all.

Laura Heitsenrether, the Jersey girl who chucked it all for Hatteras, says simply, "I tell all my friends I have never been happier. Every morning, even just to walk to the beach is absolutely gorgeous to me. Nowhere else does the beach look like this. Even when I'm surfing, the water is crystal clear. I can see straight to the bottom. And there's so much wildlife . . . jellyfish, pelicans."

It falls to David Stick, the historian, developer, and con-

The future of the island is both promising and uncertain, according to the unusual Hatteras equation. Erosion and development are balanced tenuously by the seashore park, the Outer Banks soul, and the great joy of those who want to be in this storm-buffeted paradise.

Photograph by Vicki McAllister

servationist, to put this place in perspective. "Man has made an impact on the Outer Banks, taken his best shot, often without plan or proper aim," he admits. "But the Outer Banks have survived, and if you know where to look, have changed hardly any at all."

Indeed, there seems reason not only for hope but for celebration—even if that celebration should be coupled with constant vigilance. Through it all, Hatteras has remained a special place, the keeper of the Outer Banks. "It's still where I want to live," Gee Gee Rosell says. "The compromises have been worth it." She offers the best reason for optimism: "Most people are here because they want to be. The same goes for visitors."

And there is one constant, she adds: "Mother Nature is in charge. She trumps everything."

On Hatteras, it has always been thus.

ACKNOWLEDGMENTS

A book such as this is so collaborative an effort that it seems almost fraudulent to have but one name on the cover. Among the many who assisted directly or indirectly, three persons or groups stand out.

Outer Banks historian David Stick perhaps unknowingly provided a historical framework for this book, both by graciously giving a lengthy interview and through his writings, most notably *The Outer Banks, Graveyard of the Atlantic*, and his magazine articles.

Hatteras Island tour guide and historian Danny Couch could well be called "Mr. Hatteras Island." He has made it his business to know the smallest of island stories and to gladly share them. Simply touch on a topic and this generous man is off and running. He needs to write a book himself.

Staff members of the Outer Banks History Center in Manteo, including curator KaeLi Spiers, resisted the temptation to roll their eyes at my open-ended request for "information about Hatteras Island." To them, this must have seemed akin to asking for "information about earth." Without them, I might never have discovered a valuable 2005 National Park Service study whose lead author was Barbara Garrity-Blake and whose *abbreviated* title, mind you, is *An*

Ethnohistorical Description of the Eight Villages Adjoining Cape Hatteras National Seashore and Interpretive Themes of History and Heritage. The tome contains 600 pages, not counting the 1,200 pages of 38 interview transcripts. Sometimes, good things come in big packages. Assistant curator Sarah Downing helped me track down old photographs.

A number of others generously gave of their time and expertise as well, including Nancy Molloy of the Chicamacomico Life-Saving Station, Carl Bornfriend of the Native American Museum and Natural History Center, Irene Nolan of the *Island Free Press*, and staff members of the Graveyard of the Atlantic Museum and the National Park Service. I am leaving out, of course, dozens of fishing pier owners, fishermen, business people, tourists, surfers, kite boarders, and the like, all of whom shared their love for Hatteras with me. I hope that mentioning some of their names within these pages will suffice to show my appreciation for all. Finally, other written resources, notably the works of John Morgan and Molly Perkins Harrison, proved helpful.

If any insights are to be found in this book, credit must go to these generous people. All errors of fact and perspective are mine.

My gratitude extends to graphic artist Roy Wilhelm of *Virginia Living* magazine, who once again has created a beautiful and useful map. His work always enhances these books.

Again, I am indebted to the wonderful people at John F. Blair, Publisher. The president, Carolyn Sakowski, presides over what I frequently hear from booksellers and other writers is among the very best regional publishing houses around. My experience suggests that's an understatement. My editor, Steve Kirk, again has spun my work into something I'm proud to call my work, despite my repeatedly missing deadlines this time. (Sorry, Steve.) Designer Debbie

Hampton has crafted a simply beautiful book; I loved opening up the pages as she sent them. Kim Byerly is the one who markets the book, and to her I am hugely indebted as well.

Thanks go, too, to our daughters, Jamie McAllister and Lindsay Zarse, for editing and proofreading help. Eileen Schneble assisted in proofreading. I can't leave out my parents, Bob and Joan, who inadvertently got me going on this book-writing expedition.

Last but of course first, I thank my wife, Vicki, the book's photographer and my sounding board and supporter. This is the third of these books we've done together, and the joy we get from the work is made all the better by sharing it.

BIBLIOGRAPHY

Much of the information in this book comes from the author's observations and interviews. The following were among the reference works consulted.

Barefoot, Daniel W. *Touring the Backroads of North Carolina's Upper Coast*. Winston-Salem, N.C.: John F. Blair, Publisher, 1995.

Barnes, Jay. *North Carolina's Hurricane History*. 3rd ed. Chapel Hill: University of North Carolina Press, 2001.

Butler, Lindley S. *Pirates, Privateers, and Rebel Raiders of the Carolina Coast*. Chapel Hill: University of North Carolina Press, 2000.

Carlson, Tom. *Hatteras Blues: A Story from the Edge of America*. Chapel Hill: University of North Carolina Press, 2005.

Correll, John T. "Billy Mitchell and the Battleships." *Air Force Magazine* (June 2008): 62–68.

Harrison, Molly Perkins. *Hatteras Driving Tour & Guide Book*. 3rd ed. Manteo, N.C.: One Boat Guides, 2006.

———. *It Happened on the Outer Banks*. Guilford, Conn.: Globe Pequot Press, 2005.

Impact Assessment Inc. for the U.S. Department of the Interior. *An Ethnohistorical Description of the Eight Villages Adjoining Cape Hatteras National Seashore and Interpretive Themes of History and Heritage*. National Park Service, U.S. Department of the Interior, 2005.

Khoury, Angel Ellis. *David Stick: A Life*. Manteo, N.C.: Outer Banks History Center Associates, 2003.

Kirk, Stephen. *First in Flight: The Wright Brothers in North Carolina*. Winston-Salem, N.C.: John F. Blair, Publisher, 1995.

Lee, Gabriel Francis. "Constructing the Outer Banks: Land Use, Management, and Meaning in the Creation of an American Place." Master's thesis, North Carolina State University, 2008.

Lee, Robert E. *Blackbeard the Pirate: A Reappraisal of His Life and Times*. Winston-Salem, N.C.: John F. Blair, Publisher, 1974.

MacNeill, Ben Dixon. *The Hatterasman*. Winston-Salem, N.C.: John F. Blair, Publisher, 1958. Reprinted by Publishing Laboratory of UNC Wilmington, 2008.

Morgan, John. *A Pleasant Gale on My Lee: A Notable Era in the History of the Pamlico Area and Outer Banks*. Chapel Hill, N.C.: Chapel Hill Press, 2001.

Pullen, Drew. *Portrait of the Past: The Civil War on Hatteras Island, North Carolina*. Mount Holly, N.J.: Aerial Perspective/Robert V. Drapala Publishing, 2001.

Sharpe, Bill. *Tar on My Heels*. Winston-Salem, N.C.: Tar Heels, 1946.

Stick, David. "The Cape Hatteras National Seashore." Unpublished manuscript held at the Outer Banks History Center, Manteo, N.C.

———. "Driving Down the Banks." *Our State* (June 2006): 98.

———. *Graveyard of the Atlantic: Shipwrecks of the North Carolina Coast*. Chapel Hill: University of North Carolina Press, 1952.

———. *The Outer Banks of North Carolina, 1584–1958*. Chapel Hill: University of North Carolina Press, 1958.

Stick, David, ed. *An Outer Banks Reader*. Chapel Hill: University of North Carolina Press, 1998.

Stover, Douglas. *U.S. Weather Bureau Station, Hatteras, North Carolina: Special Historic Resource Study*. Cape Hatteras National Seashore, N.C.: National Park Service, 2007.

Online Sources

"American Beginnings: The European Presence in North America, 1492–1690." *National Humanities Center, Tool-box Library: Primary Resources in U.S. History & Literature.* January 2007. http://nationalhumanitiescenter.org/pds/amerbegin/.

Chicamacomico Life-Saving Station. February 11, 2008. http://www.chicamacomico.net/.

Frisco Native American Museum & Natural History Center. 2004. http://www.nativeamericanmuseum.org/.

Island Free Press: Hatteras and Ocracoke Island News. http://islandfreepress.org/.

Midgett, John A. "Rescue of the *Mirlo*, 1918, Chicama-comico Life-Saving Station, North Carolina." *LifeSavingService.org.* 2003. http://www.lifesavingservice.org/accounts_mirlo.html.

USS Monitor *Center at the Mariners' Museum.* http://www.monitorcenter.org/.

114, 122, 136, 158, 215

Cape Hatteras Fishing Pier. *See* Frisco Pier

Cape Hatteras Indian Town. *See* Buxton

Cape Hatteras Life-Saving Station, 31, 36, 94, 122, 126, 129-30. *See also* lifesaving stations

Cape Hatteras Lighthouse: in Civil War, 54, 76, 78, 79; description of, 71, *73,* 87; erosion at, 81-82, *83,* 85; first lighthouse (1803), 74, 76, 78; as icon, 71-72, 80, 87, 89; keepers, 9, 74, 78-80, 96, 127, 247; lenses, 76, 78, *79,* 87; as marketing tool, 28, 87-88; move (1999), 82, 84-86, *84, 87,* 104; painting of, 79, 81; second lighthouse (1870), 78-89, *77, 79, 80, 83, 84, 87, 88;* shipwrecks at, 72, 186; storms at, 8, 78-79, 96; tourism and, 71-72, 89, 175, 215; as warning, 35, 74, 76, 78; in World War II, 64

Cape Hatteras National Seashore, 6, 152-61, *154, 156, 160,* 178-79, 221, 266. *See also* National Park Service

Cape Hatteras School, 108, 172, 195, 256, 258

Cape Lookout, 14, 34, 48

Cape Lookout Lightship, 34, 44, 45

Cape Point, 114, *160,* 180

Cape, the, 215. *See also* Buxton

Cape Woods. *See* Buxton Woods

Cap'n Clam charter boat, 29

Carlson, Tom, 4, 94-95, 154-55

cars on the island, early, 180, 196, 240, 246, 256. *See also* driving on the beach

Carroll A. Deering, 31-49, *33, 48,* 122

Cary, T. J., 192, 225-27, *226,* 228-29

Chappell, Oscar, *65*

charter fishing. *See* fishing, charter

Chicamacomico, 18, 54, 56, 133, 189-90, 211, 258. *See also* Rodanthe, Salvo, Waves

Chicamacomico Life-Saving Station, 119-22, *120, 123, 124,* 125, 126, 130, 132-40, *135,* 195, 198, 202. *See also* lifesaving stations

"Chicamacomico Races, the," 54, 56

churches, 51, 195

City of Atlanta, 64

Civil War, 4, 9, 17-18, 19, 51-59, *53, 55,* 68-69, 202, 216, 259

Civilian Conservation Corps, 81, 97-98, 195

Clarks. *See* Salvo

Clarksville. *See* Salvo

Coast Guard. *See* United States Coast Guard

Coast Guard magazine, 122

Coastal Area Management Act, 184

Coastland Times, 157

Colington Island, 178

Collins, William "Mojo," 86

commercial fishing. *See* fishing, commercial

Correll, John T., 143-44

Costner, Kevin, 258

Couch, Danny, 27, 29-30, 116, 255-59, *257,* 269

Creeds Hill Life-Saving Station, 36, 126, 129-30, 216. *See also* lifesaving stations

Croatans. *See* Native Americans

Crumpton, Ralph, 172, 220-21, *223,* 229, 231, 267

CSS *Virginia,* 57

Cyclops, 41

Dailey, Benjamin, 116

Dailey, Dina, 116

Dailey, Richard, 116-17, 257

Dare County, 85, 185, 215

Davenport, H. K., 76

Davis family, 133-34

De Forest, Lee, 257-58

Deal, Robert, 23, 27

DeBlieu, Jan, 197, 273-74

Decle, Chris, 259, 262

Deering, Carroll, 32, 39. *See also Carroll A. Deering*

Deuel, David, 225

development, 4, 6, 20-21, 160-61, 172, 185, 270-74, *272, 279,* 280, 282